FEMALE SERIAL KILLERS

Don Rauf

The Psychology of Serial Killers

Enslow Publishing
101 W. 23rd Street
Suite 240
New York, NY 10011
USA

enslow.com

Published in 2016 by Enslow Publishing, LLC.
101 W. 23rd Street, Suite 240, New York, NY 10011

Library of Congress Cataloging-in-Publication Data

Names: Rauf, Don, author.
Title: Female serial killers / by Don Rauf.
Description: First Edition. | New York : Enslow Publishing, 2016. | Series:
    The psychology of serial killers | Audience: Grades 9-12. | Includes
    bibliographical references and index.
Identifiers: LCCN 2015035840 | ISBN 9780766072886 (library bound)
Subjects: LCSH: Women serial murderers--Juvenile literature. |
    Women--Psychology--Juvenile literature.
Classification: LCC HV6517 .R38 2016 | DDC 364.152/32082--dc23
LC record available at http://lccn.loc.gov/2015035840

Printed in the United States of America

To Our Readers: We have done our best to make sure all websites in this book were active
and appropriate when we went to press. However, the author and the publisher have no
control over and assume no liability for the material available on those websites or on
any websites they may link to. Any comments or suggestions can be sent by e-mail to
customerservice@enslow.com.

Photo Credits: Cover, p. 1 Maksim Toome/Shutterstock.com; throughout book chrupka/
Shutterstock.com (black background), merkushev/Vasilly/Shutterstock.com (red background),
Tiberiu Stan/Shutterstock.com (brain waves activity); p. 5 © AF archive / Alamy Stock Photo;
pp. 6, 12 Enslow Publishing; p. 8 Scott Olson/Getty Images News/Getty Images; p. 10 H/O/
AFP/Getty Images; p. 17 Apic/Hulton Fine Art Collection/Getty Images; p. 19 TTstudio/
Shutterstock.com; p. 24 Tom Bastin/Flickr/CC BY 2.0; p. 26 © Dazy Rene / Bridgeman Images;
p. Apic/Hulton Collection/Getty Images; p. 32 © Geoffrey Robinson / Alamy Stock Photo; p.
39 Walter Keith Rice/Shutterstock.com; p. 42 Wikimedia Commons/ Enriqueta Martí/Public
Domain; pp.45, 81 Public Domain; p. 48 Bettmann/Corbis/AP Images; p. 54 © Steve Vidler /
Alamy Stock Photo; p. 65 Wellcome Library, London/CC BY 4.0; p. 68 Margaret Bourke-White/
The LIFE Picture Collection/Getty Images; p. 71 © Daily Mail/Rex / Alamy Stock Photo; p. 73
Press Association via AP Images; p. 77Universal History Archive/Universal Images Group/
Getty Images; p. 82 Keystone/Hulton Archive/Getty Images; p. 87 DEA / G. DAGLI ORTI/De
Agostini/Getty Images; pp. 91, 94, 97, 100, 105, 116, © AP Images; p. 109 Greater Manchester
Police/Getty Images News/Getty Images; pp. 111, 112, 114, 128, 129 Evening Standard/
Hulton Archive/Getty Images; p. 118 © David White / Alamy Stock Photo; p. 122 Florida DOC/
Getty Images News/Getty Images; p. 124 Chris Livingston/Getty Images News/Getty Images;
p. 127 DAVID DEOLARTE/AFP/Getty Images.

Contents

INTRODUCTION

When it comes to serial killing, many people may think this gruesome field is strictly for men. The fact is, throughout history, there have been a number of women who have killed repeatedly. In the United States, 8 percent of all serial killers are female, according to *The Killer Book of True Crime* by Tom and Michael Philbin.[1] Eric W. Hickey, a criminologist and author of *Serial Murderers and Their Victims*, writes that nearly 17 percent of the world's serial killers are women.[2]

Although women serial killers have been fewer in number, they have nonetheless made their mark. Murderer Aileen Wuornos brutally murdered seven men. Her life was dramatized in the motion picture *Monster*.

Because women are often assumed to be sweet and nurturing, many people can't fathom that they would kill in the cold-blooded manner of a serial killer. And it's true, these types of killers often seem harmless. They can appear to be mild-mannered housewives, jovial grandmothers, and pleasant and attractive young ladies. But underneath that façade, a madness and evil intentions may lurk.

Dr. Deborah Schurman-Kauflin, a behavioral profiler, has said that female serial killers may commit murder because they have intense feelings of helplessness and lack of control.[3] Through murder, female serial killers create power and importance in their lives. They tend to come from dysfunctional backgrounds filled with high levels of abuse and emotional cruelty, isolation, lack of stability, and abandonment.

In *Serial Murderers and Their Victims*, Eric Hickey analyzed sixty-four female serial killers to get a better understanding of their methods and motives.[4] He discovered the following:

Method	Percentage (%)
Poison	80
Shooting	20
Bludgeoning	16
Suffocation	16
Stabbing	11
Drowning	5

Motive	Percentage (%)
Money	74
Control	13
Enjoyment	11
Sex	10

With men, the main motives for serial killing are sex (even though the act of sex may or may not take place), power, manipulation, domination, and control. According to Victims of Violence, a thirty-year-old Canadian charitable organization, "men tend to be more actively violent in their killing—raping, torturing, beating, or strangling their victims— while females are usually passive and tend to favor poison."[5] Men tend to target strangers; women usually choose relatives, friends, and romantic partners.

What Is a Serial Killer?

The term "serial killer" refers to a person who kills several people over a period of time. Some criminologists define it as murdering more than three people over the course of a month or more. Some simply categorize it as the killing of two or more victims in separate events. One edition of the Federal Bureau of Investigation's (FBI's) official *Crime Classification Manual* says that for the murders to be called serial killings, there must be at least three different murders at three different locations with breaks between these events.[6] Some killers have brought victims back to the same location and have still been called serial killers.

Ernst August Ferdinand Gennat, director of Berlin's criminal police unit, may have been the first to use term "serial killer." In the 1930s, he dubbed Peter Kürten a *serienmörder,* or, in English, a serial killer. Kürten was given the nicknames the Vampire of Düsseldorf and the Düsseldorf Monster for killing nine women and girls. The term became a more common part of the language when FBI Special Agent Robert Ressler used it in reference to David Berkowitz, also known as The Son of Sam, who killed six people over a period of time in New York City from 1976 to 1977.

The 2007 mass shootings at Virginia Tech in Blacksburg, Virginia, shook the university community and the entire country. The gunman, Seung-Hui Cho, is not considered a serial killer since he snapped and killed a group of people at one time.

INTRODUCTION

Criminologists have different ways of classifying killers. A serial killer is not a mass murderer. A mass murderer is someone who snaps and kills a group of people. Student Seung-Hui Cho shot and murdered thirty-two people on Virginia Tech's campus on one day in 2007. James Holmes shot and killed twelve people and injured seventy in a rampage at a Colorado movie theater on July 20, 2012. Anders Behring Breivik killed seventy-seven people near Oslo, Norway, in 2011; sixty-nine of them were attending a youth camp.

Spree killers murder in multiple locations within a short period of time. Charles Whitman, an ex-Marine and sniper, killed his mother, his wife, and then headed to a tower at the University of Texas where he killed fourteen people. In 1997, Andrew Cunanan conducted a cross-country killing spree, murdering at least five people, including the designer Gianni Versace.

Serial killers are not usually in the same category as those who commit a crime of passion. A crime of passion killing happens as the result of a sudden strong impulse of anger or heartbreak toward someone the killer knows. Serial killers, however, often murder strangers, although family members and friends may be their victims, as well. They usually take some sort of sick pleasure in killing for killing's sake and work alone.

There are also democidal killers who murder on behalf of their government. Democide is the murder of any person or people by their government, including genocide, politicide, and mass murder. So murderous dictators and tyrants may kill many people over time, but they are not categorized as serial killers—although sometimes the lines can blur. If a ruler kills just for the thrill of it, however, that person might be deemed a serial killer.

9

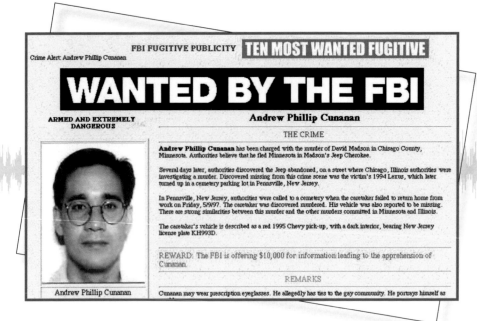

Andrew Cunanan, who murdered superstar designer Gianni Versace, is classified as a spree killer rather than a serial killer because he killed in rapid succession across a large geographic span.

Types of Female Serial Killers

In the book *Murder Most Rare* by Michael and C.L. Kelleher, the authors characterize female killers as those who act alone or those who act in partnership with at least one other person.[7] It seems that some women who murder with others become part of a cult and may even follow black magic.

Those who act alone can be separated into black widows, angels of death, sexual predators, revenge killers, and profit killers. Sometimes, murderers don't fit neatly into one category—there can be overlap.[8]

A black widow, named after the deadly spider, kills multiple spouses, partners, or other family members. An angel of death murders those who are in her care for medical attention. A sexual predator or thrill killer kills others in acts that provide some sort of sexual gratification. Occasionally, a woman will kill just for the thrill of the kill, as well. A revenge killer murders out of hate or jealousy. A profit or crime killer will take lives for profit or in the course of committing another crime.

Black widows and angels of death are the most common types of female serial killers. Revenge killers that are repeat offenders are rare because most are one-time crimes of true passion. Profit killers are somewhat rare, but they are thought to be intelligent and resourceful. One-third of all female serial killers are members of a team.

Psychopathic vs. Psychotic

Another way psychologists distinguish types of serial killers is by categorizing them as either psychopathic, also known as organized, or psychotic, also known as disorganized. Former FBI profiler Roy Hazelwood helped create this approach to better understand serial killers, according to an article in *Business Insider*.[9]

The Crime Museum in Washington, DC, explains the two types.[10] Organized killers are often clever and fairly meticulous. They plan carefully and take great care to make sure they do not leave clues as to their identity. They may track potential victims for days to decide who will be a suitable target. They are often well-equipped with tools, locations, and details on how to kill and dispose of a person. They often gain the trust of a person by faking emotions or gaining sympathy. They typically seem like normal people.

The Types and Behaviors of Serial Killers

	Organized	Disorganized
IQ	105–120 (falls within normal range)	80–95 (below average)
Social skills	Normal	Poor
Childhood	Grew up with a stable father or father figure; may have encountered physical abuse	Grew up with an abusive father or no father present; may have encountered emotional abuse
Proximity of murders to home	Moves around a lot to flee murder scenes	Commits murders around home
Living situation	Married, lives with partner, or dates	Lives alone, doesn't date
Education	Possibly attended college	Dropped out of high school
Time of activity	Daytime	Nighttime
Method of ensnaring victims	Seduction	Attack
Interaction with victims	Converses with victims	Does not consider victims to be people
Method of disposal	May dismember body after killing; disposes of remains	Leaves body behind after killing; usually does not dismember
State of crime scene	Controlled; little physical evidence left behind	Chaotic; leaves physical evidence behind
Reason for returning to scene of crime	To see the police working; interest in police work	To relive the murder

They take great pride in how they are able to kill and get away with it. These killers are psychopaths—people who suffer from chronic mental disorders and exhibit abnormal or violent social behaviors. Sometimes they will take pleasure in stumping law enforcement professionals who are trying to catch them.

Disorganized serial killers do not plan at all. Their victims just happen to be in the wrong place at the wrong time. These killers seem to murder when the moment and circumstances feel right. They usually make no effort to cover up their crimes. They are likely to leave blood, fingerprints, and the murder weapon behind; their violent acts are often messy. They move around to different locations, towns, and states to avoid capture. They typically have lower intelligence quotients (IQs) than organized killers. They may feel compelled by visions or voices they hear in their head. They usually have a form of psychosis, an extreme mental disorder in which thoughts and emotions are so impaired that they have lost their grasp on reality. They have an inability to maintain relationships, and they may be abusing drugs or alcohol. Sometimes criminals are mixed offenders, or killers who cannot be easily classified as either organized or disorganized.

Incidentally, the terms "psychopathy" and "sociopathy" are often confused and interused. Doctors don't generally diagnose using either of these terms—they use the phrase "antisocial personality disorder." Both terms refer to someone who has a continuing disregard for the rights and safety of others. A person with an antisocial personality may regularly break or flaunt the law, constantly lie or deceive others, act impulsively and not plan ahead, act irresponsibly, not meet financial obligations, and not feel any remorse or guilt. Psychologists tend to see psychopathy as genetic. The person is born that way. Sociopaths, on the other hand, are molded by their environment. Still, people with psychopathic traits may have had difficult childhoods. Psychopaths can seem totally normal and seem to form bonds with others. They can manipulate and gain trust, and while they can mimic emotion, they are unable to have any real emotions. They are often agreeable and hold down steady jobs. They are typically organized and plan their criminal activity carefully. Sociopaths are typically disorganized—they have more impulsive and chaotic actions and don't plan carefully. They tend to be nervous and easily agitated. They have difficulty holding down long-term jobs and forming attachments with others. Traits of a sociopath and psychopath can overlap in an individual.[11]

In this book, we will look at some of the more famous women serial killers according to specific categories that explain their motivations.

Chapter 1

SEXUAL PREDATORS AND THRILL KILLERS

Why do some women kill? The short answer is that they kill for the same reasons some men do. There are a variety of motives that drive women serial killers to strike. The first category to explore is the sexual predators and thrill killers. These women kill because they find a sexual thrill in murder; they often find a sadistic joy in the act itself. Here are a few women who seemed to kill mostly for the pleasure of killing.

Elizabeth Báthory

aka "The Blood Countess"

Born: **August 7, 1560**

Profession: **Countess**

Motive: **Sadism, thrill**

Date of capture: **December 19, 1610**

Date of death: **August 21, 1614**

As a member of the prominent Báthory family, Elizabeth grew up with all the privileges money could buy. She received a superior education and was well connected. Her cousin Stephen became the prince of Transylvania and later went on to rule all of Poland. She was known to be beautiful, intelligent, and fluent in German, Hungarian, and Latin. Although she spent her childhood on the Báthory estate of Ecsed in Transylvania, she was in no way related to Transylvania's other most famous resident, Vlad the Impaler, who is thought to be an inspiration for Bram Stoker's fictional character Dracula. As a young girl, Báthory had seizures and bouts of uncontrollable rage. Reportedly, one of her uncles taught her about satanism and an aunt instructed her in the joys of sadomasochism. By the age of eleven or twelve, she was engaged to marry Count Ferenc Nádasdy and become part of another aristocratic family. But before they married, the young Báthory had an affair with a peasant man and

Elizabeth Báthory suffered from seizures as a child and exhibited extreme rage. Coupled with family influences of satanism and sadomasochism, it seems she was destined to

became pregnant. To avoid scandal, the family kept Báthory seques-
tered away while pregnant and then kept her baby hidden after its
birth. Plans for the marriage continued, however, and the Countess
wed Nádasdy when she was just fourteen years old. As a soldier,
her husband often left for long stretches, so Báthory took control of
running the affairs of their estate at Csejthe Castle.

With the household under her command, Báthory's despicable
nature emerged. She seemed to take great pleasure in torturing
the staff. If a girl servant displeased her, Báthory might jam pins
under her fingernails. In the winter, she might have a woman
servant stripped and led out into the snow, where she would be
doused with cold water. In the summer, she stripped a young helper,
covered her in honey, tied her to the ground, and watched as she
was stung and bitten by insects. While her behavior was horrible
at this time, Báthory became totally unhinged when her husband
died. At age forty-four, she began spending time at her estates in
Slovakia, where she ordered her staff to capture young peasant
girls and have them brought to her house. According to numerous
accounts, she would beat, stab, mutilate, and burn them with hot
metal irons. Some say she drank their blood and even bathed in it
with the belief that it would keep her young.

Her downfall came when she started to target young women
of noble birth. As the disappearances mounted, word of her sadistic
practices eventually reached Hungary's King Matthias, who ordered
her arrest. On December 19, 1610, Báthory and four of her accomplices were captured by Hungarian authorities. Some claim that
investigators found a registry listing the names of 650 victims in
Báthory's handwriting.

Sinister activities took place inside the castle where Báthory lived with her family. The countess gleefully tortured her staff before graduating to the murder and mutilation of local girls. The Blood Countess spent her final days alone in the darkness of the castle walls. The castle itself stood empty for years and was rumored to be haunted. It was restored in 2014 and is now a popular tourist attraction.

Female Serial Killers

While three of her helpers were sentenced to death and one to life imprisonment, Báthory herself escaped execution. Because she was from such an important family, the authorities sentenced her to a lifetime in solitary confinement in January of 1611. The king also confiscated all of her property. Báthory spent the next three years in a windowless cell with her meals passed to her through a tiny slit in the wall. She died there at the age of fifty-four. [1,2,3]

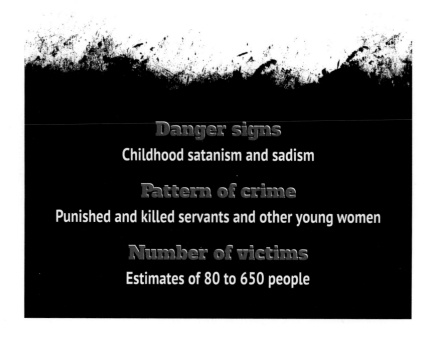

Danger signs
Childhood satanism and sadism

Pattern of crime
Punished and killed servants and other young women

Number of victims
Estimates of 80 to 650 people

Marie Delphine Lalaurie or Madam Lalaurie

Born: **March 19, 1787**

Profession: **Socialite, slaveowner**

Motive: **Lust, thrill, gain**

Date of capture: **Never caught**

Date of death: **December 7, 1842**

By all outward appearances, Delphine Lalaurie was a respected woman of the high society of New Orleans. She was known to be sweet, gracious, and captivating. Beneath the exterior of this prominent socialite, however, a monster lurked. When her terrible crimes came to light, the people of New Orleans viewed her as the devil in the form of a woman.

Lalaurie was born into a prominent New Orleans family. Her cousin was even the mayor of New Orleans from 1815 to 1820. She married three times to distinguished gentlemen. The first two seemed to die a bit prematurely after they wed. Her first husband was an influential Spanish officer, Don Ramon de Lopez y Angulo. They married when Delphine was just fourteen years old.

In 1804, while taking a voyage back to Spain, Don Ramon died. Lalaurie was expecting at the time, and during the trip, she gave birth to a daughter who was nicknamed Borquita. In 1808, she remarried. Her new husband, a Frenchman, Jean Blanque, worked as a lawyer, legislator, banker, and slave trader. He was also a friend of the notorious Gentleman Pirate, Jean Lafitte. The couple set up home in a villa in New Orleans and on a plantation along the Mississippi, where they had twenty-six slaves. Blanque and Delphine had three daughters and a son, but seven years after they wed, her husband died. Although Blanque died with a great amount of debt, Lalaurie was able to consolidate whatever assets were left by her husband and her inheritance from her parents to establish herself as a wealthy widow. After Blanque's death, Delphine emancipated one of their slaves, and reportedly she freed other slaves later on. When she was trying to prove her innocence in committing barbarous acts, she attempted to use these good deeds as evidence of her noble character.

According to some stories, Delphine met her next and last husband, the physician Louis Lalaurie, when she sought treatment for her daughter's crooked back. Lalaurie, who had arrived from Paris with a degree from the Sorbonne, announced in the local paper that he was skilled in "destroying hunches," as in hunched backs. Although sixteen years younger than Delphine, Lalaurie fell in love with her. When she was thirty-eight, the couple had a child together, and five months after his birth, they decided to marry on June 25, 1825. The young physician brought about $2,000 to the relationship, while Delphine had a fortune of about $66,000.

In 1832, Lalaurie completed a three-story mansion with attached slave quarters at 1140 Royal Street in New Orleans. Delphine apparently purchased it with her wealth and managed it under her name. After decorating the house with fine furniture, she began to hold spectacular parties. Soon after establishing this new home, the Lalauries' relationship began to fall apart, and reports of her abusing her servants spread. She kept her servants chained up.

She whipped and mutilated their bodies. According to one tale, she became enraged when a servant girl hit a snarl while combing her hair. She chased the girl with a whip, but the young woman fell to her death and was secretly buried on the property.

An investigation revealed that Lalaurie was not following laws regarding the proper treatment of slaves. Nine of her servants were taken away from her, but she was able to get them back through family connections. When a fire broke out at the mansion on April 10, 1834, the full extent of her behavior was revealed. Policemen and firefighters found the house cook chained to the stove. The seventy-year-old woman confessed to setting the blaze because she could no longer stand the torturing from her mistress and would rather die by her own hand. Bystanders wanting to make sure everyone was evacuated from the house broke into the slave quarters. They found seven slaves who were horribly mutilated, their limbs stretched or torn. One was hanging by a collar around the neck. Dr. Lalaurie told the locals that they should mind their own business, but after the tortured slaves were put on display to prove the crimes of the Lalauries, citizens stormed their home and destroyed it. As the mobs gathered, crying for the punishment of Delphine and her husband, she made it to the port, where she paid a schooner captain to take her away.

Louis Lalaurie also vanished. Reports of the time say that at least two bodies were found on the property, including that of a child. Other stories later followed saying that Delphine had blinded slaves, peeled back their skin, drilled holes in skulls, and pulled out intestines. In the end, Lalaurie was never caught. She died in Paris on December 7, 1842. In time, the mansion was restored and served as a school, a tenement, a bar, and a furniture store, among other uses.[4,5,6]

A fire broke out at Madame Lalaurie's home and revealed her dirty secrets. It is reported that some firefighters on the scene fainted when they discovered what was inside the mansion, which still stands on Royal Street.

Danger signs
Abuse began after marriage fell apart

Pattern of crime
Tortured and killed slaves

Number of victims
Several, number unknown

Jeanne Weber

aka "Madame Moulinet" or "The Ogress"

Born: **October 7, 1874**

Profession: **Housewife; worker of menial jobs**

Motive: **Power and control**

Date of capture: **May 1908**

Date of death: **July 5, 1918 (suicide)**

To many who knew her, Jeanne Weber appeared to be a small, sweet, good-tempered woman. She had humble beginnings in a small fishing village in northern France. Then at age fourteen, she moved to Paris, where she worked various menial jobs. By age nineteen, she was married, but her husband turned out to be an alcoholic. They had three children and their marriage was difficult.

In March of 1905, Weber babysat the eighteen-month-old daughter of her sister-in-law. The sister-in-law was shocked when she learned that her child had fallen ill and died suddenly while Weber was watching her. Although the child had mysterious bruises on her neck, the physician who examined her did not believe they were of any importance and listed the reason for death as natural causes.

About a week later, the same parents invited Weber back to babysit their two-year-old daughter. This child, too, died with mysterious bruising at her neck, but doctors attributed the death to

Jeanne Weber is placed under arrest—for the second time—in Paris in 1907. Having changed her identity to Madame Moulinet, Weber continued to elude punishment.

convulsions. What no one saw was that Weber was strangling these children.

Not long after, Weber's brother asked her to watch his children. He returned home to find his seven-month-old baby having a choking fit. Weber had nearly been caught in the act, but she returned the next day to finish the job. Doctors ignored the bruises around the baby's neck and blamed the death on diphtheria. Four days later, Weber's own son, seven-year-old Marcel, was found dead of "diphtheria," as well, and had the same unusual marks on his neck.

About a week after Marcel's death, Weber invited two sisters-in-law and her ten-year-old nephew, Maurice, to dinner. When the sisters-in-law stepped out to shop, Weber got Maurice in her stranglehold. The sisters-in-law, however, came back early and caught Weber in the act with a crazy, obsessed look on her face. She was arrested and went to trial for murder in January 1906. In the courtroom, Weber played the role of the grieving mother. The jury felt sympathy for her and was unwilling to find her guilty. She was acquitted and set free in February.

About a year later, Weber changed her identity to Madame Moulinet. In the town of Villedieu, she babysat for the poor Bavouzet family. On her watch, their nine-year-old son suddenly died. At first the doctor listed the cause of death as convulsions, but about a month after the death, someone identified Madame Moulinet as Jeanne Weber. Again, Weber was arrested and accused of murder. But she had a good lawyer, and a second autopsy on the boy pinned the death on typhoid. The murderess was set free. She went on to work in a children's hospital and then a children's home. Friends got her a job at the children's home trying to make amends for the injustice she had suffered. Less than a week into the job, however, Weber was caught in the act of strangling yet another child. Weber was fired, and the story was covered up.

In May of 1908, she made her way to Commercy in the east of France. Using an assumed name, she paid for a room in an inn owned by the Poirot family. One night, Weber told the innkeeper that she was afraid to sleep alone. She convinced her hosts to let her share a room with their ten-year-old son, Marcel. At about eleven o'clock, a woman named Guirlet, who was in the room next door, heard odd noises.

In her account in *The Paris Daily Mail*, Guirlet said,

I heard strange sobs and smothered screams from the next room. I got up quickly and went to M. and Mme. Poirot and told them that something was wrong. We all went together to Jeanne Weber's room and opened the door. The little boy lay dead in the bed, with his head thrown back and his eyes protruding. His tongue was bitten and had been bleeding. Jeanne Weber lay sound asleep, with one arm round the corpse and with bloodstains on her night attire. The screams and lamentations of M. and Mme. Poirot aroused the sleeper, who gazed at the dead boy in a sodden, stupefied manner, and when accused of killing him said she did not know what had happened.

The police were called and searched the room. In the bed, they found three bloodstained handkerchiefs twisted into knots. Bloodstains were also found on the floor, but an attempt had been made to wash these out.

All over France, people were captivated and horrified by the woman they called the Ogress. Readers of local news were provided with illustrations and first-person accounts of details of the case.

This time Weber was arrested for murder, and the woman who was now known throughout France as the Ogress was found to be insane and committed to an asylum. Two years into her confinement, asylum staff noticed that she would crook her fingers around invisible throats. Without any victims, she turned her will to kill on herself. She was able to strangle herself and was found dead with dried foam about her lips.[7,8]

Danger signs

Unknown

Pattern of crime

Strangled children to death

Number of victims

At least ten

Joanna Dennehy
aka "The Peterborough Ditch Murderer"

Born: **August 1992**
Profession: **Farm laborer, prostitute**
Diagnosis: **Antisocial personality disorder and paraphilia sadomasochism**
Date of capture: **April 2, 2013**
Date of death: **Still in prison**

Born in 1982 in St. Albans, Hertfordshire, England, Dennehy had, by most accounts, a normal and trouble-free childhood. She grew up in relative comfort. She was close to her sister and enjoyed playing with dolls. In school, she did well on the hockey and netball teams. Her parents had dreams that she would go on to university and maybe even become a lawyer. By fifteen, however, Dennehy was going down a more chaotic path. She was skipping school and hanging out with older boys. She started drinking and doing drugs. For a short while, she ran away to live with twenty-year-old John Treanor but then returned home. She couldn't resist the relationship, and she went back and had two children while she was still a teenager. The couple tried to make it work over the next ten years, but Dennehy cheated on Treanor and was not an attentive mother. Although she worked sporadically on farms, she didn't do much more with her life than drinking heavily.

Joanna Dennehy posed for photographs with weapons and handcuffs, which glorified her sadistic love of torture and murder.

By age twenty-seven, she was drinking up to two liters (sixty-seven ounces) of vodka a day and harming herself—slicing her arms and neck with a razor. She etched a tattoo of a star under her right eye. One day she came home to John, pulled a six-inch dagger from her knee-length boot, and stuck it into the carpet. He said she looked cold and blank. After that episode, John left for good and took their two daughters with him. Over the years, her behavior went from bad to worse. To fund her drug and alcohol abuse, she stole and worked as a prostitute.

In 2012, she was admitted to Peterborough City Hospital. A doctor there diagnosed her with antisocial personality disorder and obsessive compulsive disorder (OCD). With OCD, a person feels the need to check things repeatedly and perform routines and rituals over and over, and they have obsessive thoughts. In March of 2013, the thirty-one-year-old carried out three murders over the course of ten days. Some criminologists say that she is more correctly labeled as a spree killer rather than a serial killer because there was not a cooling-off period between killings.

Dennehy had convinced Lukasz Slaboszewski, thirty-one, that she was his girlfriend. He even texted a friend the message "life is beautiful" shortly before his death. By sending sexually suggestive texts, Dennehy persuaded Slaboszewski to meet her at a property in Peterborough. There, she stabbed him through the heart. She called a criminal friend of hers, Gary Stretch, to help get rid of the body. Stretch was a giant of a man, standing 7 feet, 3 inches (220 centimeters) tall, but around Dennehy, he was an obedient puppy and did everything she wanted. He wound up dumping the body inside a wheeled garbage bin in a town ditch. Dennehy even admitted to later showing a fourteen-year-old girl the body.

A few days later, she decided to kill her housemate John Carpenter, and she stabbed him once in the neck, twice in the heart, and three times in the chest. She told her friend Stretch, "Ooops, I've done it again." Stretch helped her again and dumped the body in the town ditch.

Men seemed to be captivated by her, including Kevin Lee, her landlord. It would prove to be a deadly attraction. Dennehy had apparently propositioned Lee with offers of kinky sex where she wanted to dress him as a woman. Lee was intrigued and agreed to meet her. When Lee met Dennehy, she stabbed him to death. He was found in a ditch, clothed in a black-sequined dress with his buttocks exposed. Dennehy and Stretch decided it was best to leave town. When she heard on the news that police were conducting a massive manhunt, she was delighted. She told Stretch she didn't want to stop killing and that she was excited the police were looking for her.

She continued her pattern of violence. Dennehy stabbed Robin Bereza from behind and less than ten minutes later, Dennehy stabbed John Rogers, leaving the man for dead and stealing his dog. Although she gravely injured these men, they survived.

David Wilson, professor of criminology at Birmingham City University, described Dennehy and Stretch's relationship as a *folie à deux,* or shared psychosis. They created an unreal world where horrible behaviors seemed acceptable. It is possible she suffered from paraphilia sadomasochism, a condition in which sexual excitement is derived from pain and humiliation. It is also possible that she is unable to feel the normal range of human emotions.

After being arrested on April 2, 2013, Dennehy said she killed to see if she was as cold as she felt. She said she had a lack of respect for human life. Dennehy pleaded guilty to the murders on November 18, 2013, and was sentenced to life in prison on February 28, 2014. [9,10,11]

She is only the third woman in British history deemed too dangerous to ever be released.

Danger signs
Drinking, OCD, antisocial behavior

Pattern of crime
Lured and killed men

Number of victims
Three

Chapter 2

PROFIT OR CRIME KILLERS

Another category of women serial killers are profit killers, also known as crime killers. Profit killers usually murder to gain money or material wealth. Sometimes they team up with others, but often they act alone. Sometimes they get pleasure out of killing, but the primary drive appears to be a desire to make a profit.

Lavinia Fisher

Born: 1793
Profession: Hotel owner
Motive: Gain
Date of capture: Spring 1819
Date of death: February 18, 1820
(executed)

Specific information about Lavinia Fisher's childhood is unknown, but her infamous place in history begins when she married John Fisher, a convicted bank robber. In the early 1800s, she and her husband opened the Six Mile Wayfarer House, which was located six miles (ten kilometers) outside of Charleston, South Carolina. Rumors started to grow around the couple as men would check into the inn and then mysteriously disappear. Some claimed that the attractive Lavinia would invite male guests to dinner. Over a hearty meal and perhaps some drinks, Lavinia would flirt and find out about a guest's background and job. If a guest seemed to be carrying money on his trip, she would offer him a cup of tea before sending him off to bed. The tea was either spiked with a drug to put the guest into a deep sleep or it was lethally poisoned. As the story goes, either John Fisher would then slip into the room and stab the victim or Lavinia would pull a lever that would dump the victim from his bed and through a trapdoor in the room. The person would tumble through a chute and

Local authorities investigated reports of men vanishing, but Lavinia and John were well-liked in the community, and at first found nothing suspicious going on at their establishment. They were found out after a fur trader named John Peeples checked in one day in 1819. At first, Peeples was told there was no room, but he should join Lavinia for dinner. She seemed friendly—in fact, she seemed too friendly. As the night progressed, Lavinia must have gathered that a fur trader could be carrying some money with him. At some point in the meal, she told Peeples that they found a spare room for him to stay in. She offered him the customary cup of tea. Fortunately, Peeples didn't like tea. When Lavinia wasn't looking, he dumped his cup. Suspicious of the situation, Peeples stayed up all night in a chair facing his door in his room. At some point in the night, he suddenly saw his bed collapse and a trapdoor opening to a cellar below, where he spied John Fisher clutching an axe. Peeples scrambled out a window and hightailed it to Charleston to tell the police.

When the Fishers were arrested, lawmen discovered that they were part of a large gang of highwaymen, and they let outlaws use the inn as a hideout. A grave was found a couple of hundred yards from the Six Mile Wayfarer House containing the remains of two humans, but it was hard to make a case for murder against the Fishers. When they went on trial in 1819, the Fishers were tried for highway robbery and not murder, but highway robbery was punishable by execution. They pleaded innocent but were found guilty. They were given a chance to appeal their case, and their appeal would come to court in January 1820.

In September of 1819, they tried to escape prison. Making a rope from blankets, John lowered himself out a window, but it

Lavinia Fisher was held in the Charleston jail with her husband, John. The couple was condemned to death by gallows, and Lavinia did not go quietly.

snapped before he could reach the ground. He could have fled without Lavinia, but he stayed behind for his wife. The two were then kept in a cell under much tighter security. A court eventually denied their appeal, and the husband and wife were condemned to hang on February 4, 1820. Lavinia argued that it was against the law to execute a married woman, so the judge ordered that John be put to death first—then Lavinia would no longer be married.

On the day they were to be hanged, many of the fine local ladies and gentlemen of Charleston attended. Lavinia and John were led to the gallows in white robes, which may have led to a rumor that Lavinia was hanged in her wedding dress. According to reports, John peacefully accepted his fate, but Lavinia raged against her execution. One historian wrote: "She stamped in rage and swore with all the vehemence of her amazing vocabulary, calling down damnation on a governor who would let a woman swing. The crowd stood shocked into silence, while she cut short one curse with another and ended with a volley of shrieks." Lavinia's last words are remembered to this day, "If anyone has a message for Hell, give it to me, and I'll carry it!" The twenty-seven-year-old then jumped off the scaffold herself.[1,2]

Danger signs

Unknown

Pattern of crime

Poisoning or stabbing inn guests

Number of victims

Unconfirmed

Enriqueta Martí,
aka *"The Vampire of Barcelona"*

Born: **1868**

Profession: **Maidservant, prostitute**

Motive: **Gain**

Date of capture: **February 27, 1912**

Date of death: **May 12, 1913**

Coming from the countryside of Catluña, Spain, Enriqueta Martí set off to the big city of Barcelona to better her life. The city was swiftly growing and teeming with people, but there was also lots of poverty and people living in the streets. Martí thought herself lucky to find work as a maid with several bourgeois families. Because she was young and good-looking, she found she could make even more money as a prostitute.

For a brief time, it seemed that Martí might abandon her wicked ways and follow a more traditional path. In 1895, she wed Joan Pujaló. Although he disapproved of her prostitution, she would continually slip back into that trade. They tried hard to make the relationship work, coming together and breaking up about six times. Because prostitution bought her the luxuries she craved, such as a nice apartment and pretty clothes, she refused to give it up.

In 1909, Martí opened her own brothel. Her business attracted many of the well-to-do of Barcelona, and some of them had

Enriqueta Martí was known as the Vampire of Barcelona because she convinced wealthy ladies that drinking children's blood would cure certain ailments.

perverse desires to which she was willing to cater—for a price. She learned that some wanted to have interactions with children. So during the day, she would dress as a pauper. In her rags, she would walk among the poor people of Barcelona. When she spied a child who was unattended, she would abduct them. She was able to kidnap many children, ages five to fifteen, who she would then provide to pedophiles who would pay her a substantial sum. Some clients may have murdered the children. At night, she would shed her beggar's garments and dress in the finest clothes. Often, she would visit a casino or attend the theater dressed in the most elegant fashions of the day.

A certain group of distinguished ladies of Barcelona believed that creams and elixirs made from children might make them live longer and give them more youthful looks. Martí claimed to her privileged clientele that drinking a child's blood could cure them of tuberculosis. So Martí began to make the products by killing children for their fat, blood, and bones—ingredients in these gruesome and expensive concoctions. Marc Pastor, a crime scene investigation (CSI) detective based in Barcelona, said that Martí was a psychopath who enjoyed what she did.

At the end of July 1909, an organized protest of the working classes against sending conscripted troops, or men forced to serve in the military, into Morocco occurred in Barcelona. The protests erupted into bloody clashes, and this time was dubbed the Tragic Week. Because tensions were running high in the city, more police were sent into the streets. During this time, Martí's brothel was discovered. She was accused of prostituting children, but because she now had strong connections with the wealthy society of Barcelona, she was able to escape punishment and return to her nefarious ways. Over the next three years, many more children disappeared, but the children were from poor families, and the police made little effort to find them.

When Teresita Guitart Congesta vanished on February 10, 1912, the people had enough. The public outcry was great, and the police had to respond. Seven days later, a neighbor spied a girl looking from a window of Martí's home. With suspicions aroused, she told another neighbor what she saw, and the police were notified. When they entered Martí's home, they found Teresita and another young girl name Angelita. Martí told police that she was trying to help the poor and starving Teresita. She also said that Angelita was her daughter. But police soon learned the truth. She had lured the girls to her home with a promise of candies. When she had them in her home, she told them their parents were dead.

On one occasion when Martí left the house, the girls had discovered a sack that contained a girl's bloody clothes and a boning knife stained with blood. Angelita told police that she saw Martí kill a five-year-old boy on her kitchen table. Upon deeper inspection of the apartment, the authorities not only found the bag with bloody clothing and the knife, they found another bag with at least thirty human bones that appeared to be from children, as well as more clothing. As they made their way further into the home, they uncovered a hidden room that was a fancier, comfortable lounge with nice boys' and girls' clothes in it. But in here was a more gruesome discovery—fifty jars, washbowls, and pitchers containing human remains, bones, and dried blood. There was also evidence showing that these ingredients were being mixed and put into vials or pots of salve.

Teresita Congesta was one of the lucky girls to be saved from Martí's clutches.

As the evidence mounted, police were sent to another home that Martí kept. In spaces behind the walls and in the ceiling, they found the remains of several children. In yet another residence of hers, police discovered children's blood, hair, and bits of human bodies in vases and jars. She eventually confessed that she used children's bodies to make healing creams, ointments, and potions. Here, Martí also kept what appeared to be a recipe book of potions, precisely and beautifully handwritten. In addition, Martí had written down all the names of prominent citizens in Barcelona who had used her services. The police, however, protected the names of these wealthy clients from the public and said the list was only people who were tricked or swindled by Martí.

Finally, Martí was arrested and put in jail. As tales of her grisly acts spread, she became known as the Vampire of Barcelona. Although jailers stopped her once from committing suicide, she did not live to go on trial. Some claim she died of uterine cancer, but in reality, it may be that her prison mates beat her to death.[3,4]

Danger signs:
Unknown

Pattern of crime:
Luring children, killing them, and using them for expensive creams

Number of victims:
At least ten

Delfina and Maria de Jesus Gonzalez
aka "Las Poquianchis"

Born: Possibly 1912 for Delfina and unknown for Maria

Profession: Brothel owners

Motive: Gain

Date of capture: January 14, 1964

Date of death: October 17, 1968, for Delfina; unknown for Maria

Brought up in Juanacatlán, Mexico, the sisters Delfina and Maria de Jesus Gonzalez were poor. Their father, who worked with the rural police, was strict and forbade his daughters from wearing makeup, lipstick, or risqué clothing. After their father shot a man during an argument, the family moved to a small village called San Francisco del Rincon. As young women, they opened a saloon to earn some money. They made just enough to get by. To improve their lot in life, they decided to turn to prostitution. By bribing officials with money and sex, the sisters were able to open several houses of prostitution throughout Mexico. They would search the countryside for the prettiest young women and then trick the poor girls and offer them jobs as waitresses and maids in the big city. Sometimes they would place help wanted ads in the papers to lure

The Gonzalez sisters, Delfina (*top*) and Maria (*bottom*), were imprisoned for the deaths of eleven people. The sisters ran a sex slave ring through which authorities estimated two thousand girls passed.

women in. Once in their grasp, the sisters would force the young women to work as prostitutes and threaten to harm them if they disobeyed.

Delfina's son, known as El Tepo, and her lover, an army captain nicknamed the Black Eagle, served as the muscle by capturing women and keeping them in line. They often gave the women heroin or cocaine to keep them subdued. The poor young women were treated as sexual slaves. The sisters especially liked to find virgins because they earned the highest amount of money from customers. The women were often raped and beaten. If they became pregnant, they were not allowed to stay that way for long. They would be beaten until they lost their babies, and their fetuses would be buried. If a girl lost her good looks or became too ill from lack of nourishment, sexually transmitted disease, or another sickness, she would be locked away until she starved to death. Sometimes, the other working girls were told to beat their weakened coworker to death with sticks.

Some customers who came with large amounts of money also met untimely ends. When their bodies were found by police later, the sisters said they died because the food didn't agree with them. Many women and men disappeared throughout the 1950s and into the early 1960s, but no one bothered the women because too many councilmen, policemen, soldiers, and officials enjoyed the services provided by the sisters.

Along the way, the sisters bought a bar called El Poquianchi, and townspeople began to refer to them as Las Poquianchis. In 1963, El Tepo got in a fight with local cops who wound up shooting him dead. The enraged Delfina wanted revenge for her son, and she sent the Black Eagle to kill those responsible, which he did. But the incident now pitted some of the police against the sisters.

In January of 1964, Catalina Ortega, one of the prostitutes, escaped. She told her tale of abuse and captivity to the Judicial Police office in Leon, Guanajuato. Luckily, these police were not under the control of the sisters. Word spread quickly of the sisters' reported horrific deeds. With a search warrant in hand, police raided the sisters' Loma del Angel ranch. The police were greeted by the two seemingly harmless sisters dressed in black—still mourning the death of Delfina's son. As villagers gathered outside yelling that the sisters be lynched, the authorities found dozens of starving, dirty women locked in a room. The women showed them bloodied patches of ground where they said they would find the bodies of many who were murdered. All in all, they uncovered the bodies of eighty women, eleven men, and several fetuses.

During their trial, dozens of ex-prostitutes came forward with tales of how they were captured by the sisters and held against their will. Many were raped and forced to give the money they earned to the sisters. The two sisters were accused of murdering scores of women and men. Although villagers called for their death, the judge sentenced each woman to forty years in prison.

On October 17, 1968, Delfina died when a bucket of cement accidentally hit her in the head in prison. Maria, however, was eventually freed, although it is unknown why. She disappeared and was never heard from again.[5,6]

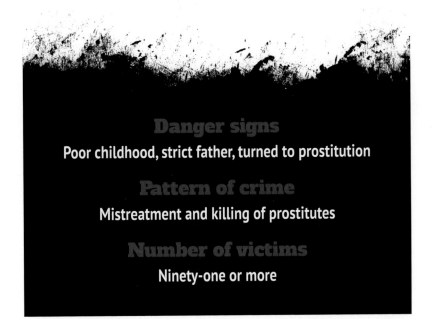

Danger signs

Poor childhood, strict father, turned to prostitution

Pattern of crime

Mistreatment and killing of prostitutes

Number of victims

Ninety-one or more

Chapter 3

ANGELS OF DEATH

As is the case with the other categories in this resource, the serial killers who fall into the angels of death category aren't exclusively women, but many are. Angels of death work in hospitals or senior-living homes and find exhilaration by controlling the life and death of their patients. They often like the attention they receive for caring for the very people they are killing.

Amelia Dyer
aka "The Angel Maker"

Born: **1839, date unknown**
Profession: **Baby farmer**
Motive: **Gain**
Date of capture: **April 4, 1896**
Date of death: **June 10, 1896
(executed)**

In Victorian England, Amelia Dyer delivered, fostered, and adopted illegitimate babies for money. She would tell people that if they gave her the baby and some money, she would make sure the baby was adopted or she would raise it herself. In reality, she simply killed the infants. Remarkably, she was able to get away with this gruesome practice for thirty years.

Coming from a relatively comfortable background, Dyer was able to attend school—a luxury not afforded to most girls at this time. As a youngster, she saw her mother lose her mind and writhe in pain when she contracted typhus fever. As she became a young adult, Dyer turned to a career in nursing. She had the right temperament—one had to be hearty and emotionless to deal with all the suffering. In 1864, twenty-six-year-old Dyer became pregnant. She could not continue work, so she left nursing. When her husband died, she realized the difficulties of raising a child alone. Dyer heard of Ellen Dane, a baby farmer who—for a fee—took in women

---WANTED---

AMELIA DYER
BABY MURDERER

Amelia Dyer (born 1838) was a midwife, who knew that once her fee had been paid mothers were rarely interested in their infants' welfare (and fathers less so) she at first tended to neglect sicklier babies, allowing them to die of starvation, but over time assumed the practice of simply strangling babies as soon as she had pocketed the fee and the mother had departed. It was peace of mind they were paying for after all, the children's welfare barely seemed to matter. Killing them was simply cheaper.

Suspicions were raised when the tiny corpses of her victims were found in the Thames, their throats bound with white dressmaking tape. When detectives raided her home they said it stank of decomposing bodies.

While Amelia Dyer pleaded guilty to a single murder, she had committed many more. Perhaps up to 400, placing her among the most prolific killers of all time. She was hanged at Newgate Prison on Wednesday, June 10, 1896.

 DEAD OR **ALIVE**

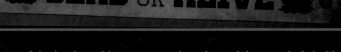

Dyer tricked vulnerable young mothers into giving up their babies when they could no longer afford to care for them. Instead of finding good homes for the babies, Dyer murdered them.

who were having illegitimate children and offered the additional service of adopting. Dyer decided to farm her own child out.

Dyer also wanted her daughter out of the way as she began operating her own business. She created smart, well-written advertisements telling women that their child would be well-looked after in a loving and caring home. But instead of helping the children, she would collect a fee from the mothers and then strangle the babies by taking out some tape, tying the tape around the baby's neck, and pulling. When the baby stopped breathing, she would wrap the baby in a package of brown paper. She would tie the bundle up with string and drop it in the Thames with a brick. She said that she felt peaceful when she placed the little bodies in the river.

The actual killing of the child might have given Dyer a godlike power over the babies. She was sending them to their maker. The more she did it, the more desensitized she may have become. She had some sort of perverted maternal perspective, according to Dr. Allan Beveridge, a consultant psychiatrist from Queen Margret Hospital, on the TV Show *Lady Killers*. While Dyer disposed of many of the babies right away by throwing them into rivers, she also kept many until they decomposed so they could not be traced back to her.

By the end of the 1860s, the scale of the nationwide infanticide epidemic could no longer be ignored, and other baby farmers were being arrested for murder. Amelia Dyer continued working under pseudonyms to help keep her operation and history a secret. For a while, she stopped baby farming and worked in an asylum. She felt the police might catch her. In 1872, she married and settled down to a standard family life. But her husband lost his job, and she went back to baby farming full time. Her practices came under police scrutiny when they found that four children under her care had died.

She took a massive laudanum overdose in an attempt to kill herself, but she didn't die. For her neglectful care of these children, she was given a six-month sentence with hard labor.

In 1890, Dyer began targeting wealthier people to try and make more money. A young governess discovered that Dyer was not what she seemed. The governess had gotten pregnant by the master of the house and turned the baby over to Dyer. When the governess returned to give Dyer her final payment and see her child one more time, Dyer presented her with a child that was not hers. Then the governess repeatedly tried to get back her child. She contacted the police, who went to investigate. Dyer put off the police time and time again. She told them that the governess's baby had been adopted. Feeling hounded and hunted, she had a period of feeling completely irrational, and she threatened suicide. When a doctor was called in, she flew at him and said she was hearing voices. She also said that the birds told her to do it. She was committed to an asylum.

In a short time, Dyer was out and back in business. She brought a woman she had met, Jane Smith, in to help, but Dyer treated her as a servant. Now Dyer acquired infants at a furious speed. Jane Smith had no idea where the infants were going, and she began to feel uneasy about the situation. One day, Smith noticed a terrible smell coming from one of the cupboards. Dyer cleaned the cupboard and left with a parcel while saying she was taking clothes to the pawn-shop. Soon after, on March 30, 1896, a Thames bargeman saw the package and hooked it out of the river. Inside the parcel was a dead baby with a name and address. One of Dyer's old addresses was left in the package with one of her aliases—Mrs. Thomas. He reported it to the police, who found a house at that address bulging with evidence of the adoption of babies. Through some investigative work, they traced the package back to Dyer.

Arrested at age fifty-eight, Dyer was taken to Reading police station, where she tried to commit suicide. On April 10, 1896, a carpetbag containing two bodies were discovered in the Thames, and fifty babies total were pulled out of the river. They were identified as Dyer's victims because of the tape around the necks. She took full responsibility for the crimes and confessed to all the murders. In an attempt to avoid execution, she pled insanity and said there was insanity in her family. She finally confessed that she murdered the babies and grew to like the act of murdering. She said she "used to like them with a tape around their neck." She was hanged at Newgate Prison on June 10, 1896.[1,2]

Danger signs
Unknown

Pattern of crime
Falsely adopted babies and then killed them

Number of victims
Estimated to be as many as four hundred

Maria Catherina Swanenburg

aka "Good Me"

Born: **September 9, 1839**

Profession: **Caregiver who attended to children and the sick**

Motive: **Gain**

Date of capture: **December 1883**

Date of death: **April 11, 1915 (in prison)**

Until she was in her forties, Maria Catherina Swanenburg led a rather ordinary, uneventful life. She appeared to be a good mother and housewife. When she was twenty-nine, she married Johannes van der Linden, and the couple had five sons and two daughters. Swanenburg would sometimes give her name as van der Linden, but she often used her maiden name. In her early forties, she began offering her services to the poor residents of her town, Leiden, Holland. She told families that she was interested in tending to children and the sick. In addition to bathing and feeding those in her care, she would perform all housekeeping duties, such as cooking, running errands, and cleaning house. Her generosity and caring spirit earned her the nickname of Goede Mie, or Good Me.

She started to take out insurance policies on those in her care. She said she wanted to have money to take care of any funeral expenses—just in case. Often, her patients would become more ill under her care, and it took some time before people discovered that Good Me was the cause. She slowly poisoned her patients with arsenic. Apparently, she first tried her wicked scheme out on her own parents, whom she poisoned to death in the early 1880s. Then she secured employment in different households. Families appreciated how attentive she was as their loved ones became sicker and sicker. She would sit at their bedsides and lovingly feed them poison-laced meals and drinks. Sometimes she would laugh and take pleasure at the torment of those whom she was slowing killing. In total, she killed at least twenty-seven people and seriously sickened forty-five. For many of the survivors, life was a hardship as the arsenic left them crippled and walking around Leiden on crutches.

Swanenburg kept careful records of her intended victims. She gained confidence in her cruel ways. She even threatened one man who was burying a relative who had been in her care. She told him, "It will be your turn in one month." The man should have taken her seriously because she made sure her prediction came true.

Her wicked ways were finaly discovered when she went to the Groothuizen family. They caught the murderess in the act of poisoning their food. After she was arrested on December 15, 1883, investigators became suspicious of all the deaths that had occurred under her watch. When bodies were exhumed and examined, the horrible truth came to light. In a courtroom description, Swanenburg was described as "a pale and ugly woman, with no expression of intelligence." Although evidence showed she had killed at least twenty-seven people, she was only found guilty of killing her final three victims. She was sentenced to a life of confinement in a correctional facility, where she died at age seventy-six.[3,4]

Danger signs:
Began taking out insurance policies
on those under her care

Pattern of crime:
Slowly poisoning patients

Number of victims:
At least twenty-seven

Jane Toppan
aka "Jolly Jane" or "The Nightmare Nurse"

Born: **1857, date unknown**
Profession: **Nurse**
Motive: **Thrill, lust**
Date of capture: **October 1901**
Date of death: **August 17, 1938**

Jane Toppan had an unhappy and troubled childhood. Born as Honora Kelley in Massachusetts, Toppan lost her mother to consumption, or tuberculosis, when she was young. Her father, Peter, not only drank excessively and had violent outbursts, but he also appeared to have mental problems. Townspeople called him Kelley the Crack because of his mad behavior. After his wife's death, Peter Kelley took Honora and her sister, Delia, to an orphanage called the Boston Female Asylum, and the management there determined the girls had been neglected and abused. When Honora reached age seven or eight, Ann C. Toppan took her as her foster child and indentured servant and renamed her Jane Toppan.

By most accounts, Jane developed a deep-rooted envy and hatred of Ann Toppan's biological daughter, Elizabeth. Elizabeth seemed to have it all. Meanwhile, Jane's real sister, Delia, was taken in as a foster child in another family. She eventually turned to prostitution and died a poor alcoholic.

Jane Toppan was adopted from her abusive father into a good home. However, she was unable to shake her past and jealousy of her adoptive sister, Elizabeth. Toppan used her position as a nurse to inflict abuse upon her patients, among others.

At school, Jane tried to put forth a vivacious personality to gain friends, but classmates would often grow tired of her telling false tales. When she was officially freed of her servant obligations, Jane was allowed to remain in the Toppan home. Elizabeth tried to be kind to her and help her as much as she could.

At age twenty-eight, Jane decided to pursue a career as a nurse and got training at Cambridge Hospital in Boston. Here, she gained the nickname Jolly Jane from her patients because of her outgoing and happy personality—and that name stuck with her later as her devious deeds were exposed. Her coworkers were not as enamored with her. Several times, she was caught telling lies about her past or gossiping about others on staff.

As she became attached to some patients, she wanted them to stay in the hospital. She would administer drugs to them to keep them ill longer. Treating patients as her guinea pigs, she began experimenting on them with morphine and atropine, an active ingredient in the poisonous plant called nightshade or belladonna. As her patients drifted in and out consciousness, Jane would sometimes climb into bed with them. Jane described how she got a sexual thrill as she held patients who slipped toward death, then revived, and then passed away. She seemed to slide her patients between life and death, toying with them, before finally letting them go. One patient who survived recalled how Jane gave her a bitter-tasting medicine, and as she slipped into a haze, she recalled Jane getting into bed with her and kissing her all over the face.

It's estimated that more than a dozen of Jane's patients died under mysterious circumstances at Cambridge Hospital. Yet when she applied for work at Massachusetts General Hospital in 1889, she received glowing recommendations from doctors she had worked with. Again, patients started to die with no real explanation. A year after she started at Massachusetts General, however, she was dismissed for leaving the ward without permission. Cambridge Hospital took her back, but she didn't last long there. She was suspected of recklessly administering opiates and fired. She turned to work as a private nurse and did quite well even though many of her employers thought she was a liar and petty thief.

Jane took her deeds to a new level when she poisoned her landlord because she thought he was too fussy. She moved in with his elderly wife, but in two years she tired of her as well and murdered her in the same fashion.

Her adoptive sister, Elizabeth, still cared for her, and in 1899, she invited Jane to stay with her at her vacation home in Cape Cod. Elizabeth took ill soon after Jane arrived. Jane had not stopped hating Elizabeth despite her kindnesses, and she was slipping strychnine into her food. After disposing of Elizabeth, she took a job tending to an ailing seventy-year-old woman and killed her off. She reconnected with an old friend named Myra Conners. Myra worked as a dining matron at a theological school. Jane thought she'd like that job, so she killed her old friend and told Myra's employers that Myra was planning to take a leave of absence and was going to recommend Jane as her replacement. The school hired her. Again, her poor work performance got her fired. She decided to poison the housekeeper where she lived to try to get her job. Jane poisoned her just enough to make her sick and convince the landlords that the housekeeper was a drunk. Her plan worked, and they hired Jane.

Now her poisonings were escalating. Jane rented a cottage and poisoned the landlady there. The landlady was Mattie Davis, and she left behind her husband and two daughters. Jane told the new widower that she would take care of him and his family until they recuperated from the loss. Within weeks, however, they were all dead.

She then set in motion a plan to win the heart of her foster sister's husband, Oramel. Because she felt Oramel's sister might interfere with her plan, Jane killed her. Then she poisoned Oramel just enough so she could nurse him back to health and prove her devotion. But Oramel asked her to leave. In the meantime, relatives of Mattie Davis asked to have the bodies exhumed and examined.

Jane Toppan often administered morphine to patients, which allowed them to drift into unconsciousness so she could revive them and be their savior.

When a toxicology report showed that one of the daughters had been poisoned, Jane was arrested for murder on October 26, 1901.

In time, she was officially charged with four counts of murder. She was found not guilty by reason of insanity and committed for life to the Taunton Insane Hospital. She eventually confessed to killing eleven people and admitted that the killing fed some sort of sexual impulse. Later, she told her lawyer she had actually killed thirty-one people. In a confession she gave to the newspaper the *New York Journal*, Jane said that she had tricked everyone with her insanity plea and she killed for the sheer pleasure it gave her. Although she thought she would somehow be able to convince the institution to let her go in due time, she spent the next thirty-seven years in the mental institution and lived until the ripe old age of eighty.[5,6]

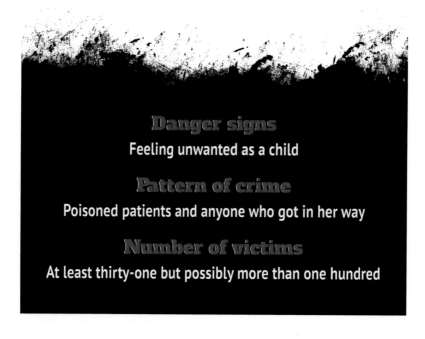

Danger signs
Feeling unwanted as a child

Pattern of crime
Poisoned patients and anyone who got in her way

Number of victims
At least thirty-one but possibly more than one hundred

Miyuki Ishikawa

aka "The Demon Midwife"

Born: **1897**

Profession: **Hospital director in the Kotobuki maternity ward**

Motive: **Gain**

Date of capture: **January 15, 1948**

Date of death: **Unknown**

Born in Kunitomi, toward the southern tip of Japan, Miyuki Ishikawa was a good student and graduated from the University of Tokyo. She married Takeshi Ishikawa, became an experienced midwife, and landed a job as the hospital director in a maternity ward. If conditions were different, Ishikawa may have led a fairly normal life. As World War II was drawing to a close in 1944, many couples were having children but didn't have the financial means to take care of them. There was also a huge lack of social and charitable services at this time.

Ishikawa saw that these babies would have to grow up under great hardship. She decided it would be best for all concerned if these babies died. Through neglect and starvation, scores of infants died under Ishikawa's instructions. Many midwives working at the hospital left in disgust. Ishikawa and her husband also informed some parents that they would give them death certificates for their children and

As World War II drew to a close, scores of children in Japan were left in orphanages. Disturbed by the idea that the babies she delivered would lead difficult lives, Miyuki Ishikawa killed them.

free them of the financial burden if they would pay them one large sum. She explained how she was saving them money in the long run.

The bodies of the babies were not buried in a traditional manner but disposed of secretly so as not to call attention to the large scale of the killings. Police, however, found five baby corpses, which led them to Ishikawa. Autopsies confirmed that the infants had not died from natural causes. Police increased their efforts to find children who seemed to have disappeared from the hospital.

They found forty infant corpses at a mortician's house and thirty more under a temple.

Ishikawa, her husband, and accomplices were arrested on January 15, 1948, and put on trial. In court, Ishikawa defended herself by saying these babies had been deserted by their parents, so the parents should be the ones held responsible for their deaths. In the end, the Tokyo court viewed her deeds as a crime of omission, which means she was guilty by failing to act. She failed to care for these babies, and she let them die. The public labeled her the Demon Midwife, but she only received a sentence of eight years, which was later reduced to four. This type of neglect killing, however, is thought to have led to the limited legalization of abortion in Japan.[7,8]

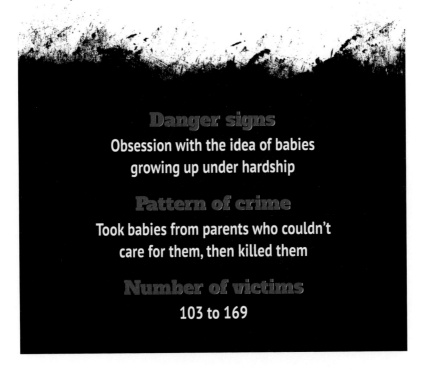

Danger signs
Obsession with the idea of babies
growing up under hardship

Pattern of crime
Took babies from parents who couldn't
care for them, then killed them

Number of victims
103 to 169

Beverly Allitt
aka "The Angel of Death"

Born: **October 4, 1968**

Profession: **Nurse**

Daignosis: **Munchausen syndrome by proxy**

Date of capture: **November 1991**

Date of death: **Serving thirteen life sentences**

Beverly Allitt had signs of the mental disorder Munchausen syndrome at an early age, including faking medical problems to get attention. She would wear bandages and casts but never show anyone her actual injuries. She often visited doctors and complained of ailments, but they could find nothing wrong with her. She convinced a surgeon to remove her perfectly healthy appendix, and her scar was slow to heal because she picked at it.

She was eventually accepted to Grantham College in Lincolnshire, England, where she studied to be a nurse. Stories of odd behavior followed her during her training. She was suspected of smearing feces on a wall at a nursing home. A boyfriend at the time said she was deceptive, manipulative, and aggressive. She made false claims of being pregnant and raped. She often missed work and complained about a range of ailments, including gallbladder pain, headaches, and urinary tract infections. Despite questionable behavior, she was able to land a job in the children's ward at Grantham and Kesteven Hospital in Lincolnshire in 1991.

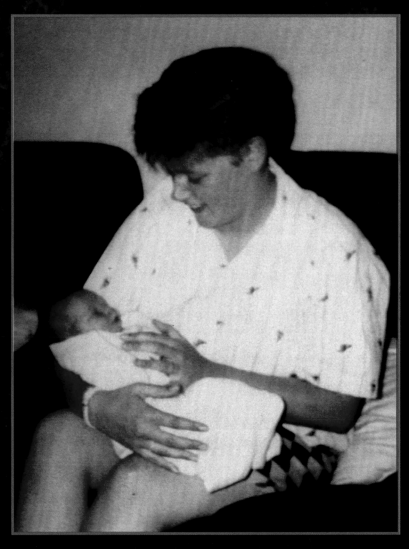

Beverly Allitt suffered from several psychological disorders, including Munchausen syndrome. Perhaps it was her love of hospitals that drove her to become a nurse.

When seven-month-old Liam Taylor was suffering from a respiratory infection, his parents brought their son to the hospital on February 21, 1991. Allitt assured the worried parents that their boy was in good hands and to head home and get some rest. The next day, they learned that Liam had a respiratory emergency but was fine. Allitt volunteered to put in extra time and tend to the boy overnight. This time, Liam stopped breathing. Nurses who worked with Allitt were puzzled as to why equipment alarms did not sound. Allitt called the emergency medical staff, but it was too late. The boy had suffered severe brain damage, and the parents decided to take him off life support.

Just two weeks later, another boy—eleven-year-old Timothy Hardwick—suffered a similar fate. A few victims followed whom doctors were able to resuscitate, but there were always unexplainable signs. One boy had mysteriously high levels of insulin; a young girl had an odd puncture mark under her arm. When twins Katie and Becky Phillips were put under Allitt's care, they were two months old and weak from a premature delivery. Soon Becky was cold to the touch, and Allitt said she had low blood sugar. Becky was sent home, but overnight she had convulsions and died. Under Allitt's attentive care, Katie stopped breathing. She was revived but then suffered a similar attack. The oxygen deprivation resulted in partial paralysis, cerebral palsy, and some loss of sight and hearing. The parents, however, thought Allitt had saved their baby's life. They were so thankful that they made Allitt the child's godmother.

There were a few more close calls for children in Allitt's care, and then fifteen-month-old Claire Peck died on April 22, 1991. She was asthmatic and suffered a heart attack under Allitt's watch. She was successfully revived once, but when left alone again with

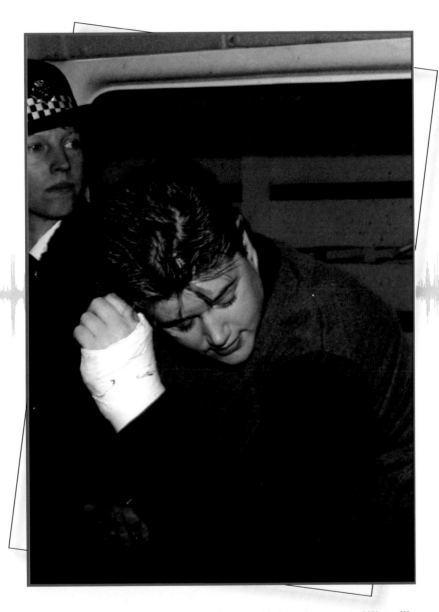

Sentenced to thirteen concurrent terms of life imprisonment, Allitt will serve a minimum of thirty years. This means she could be released in 2022, when she will be fifty-four years old.

Allitt, she died of another attack. With so many episodes recorded under Allitt's care, one doctor began to investigate and found the drug lignocaine was in the baby's system. This drug is given for cardiac arrest but never to babies. This led the hospital to contact the police.

Examining the records of other children under Allitt's care, they found more suspicious activity—many were given high doses of insulin. When records were checked, nursing logs and a key to the insulin refrigerator were found to be missing. Allitt was arrested and convicted on May 23, 1993, and given thirteen life sentences for murder and attempted murder. While imprisoned at Rampton Secure Hospital in Nottingham, England, Allitt has tried to injure herself by eating broken glass and pouring boiling water on her hand. Some of her victims' families have complained that this hospital is comfortable and not like a prison in the least. They feel she is not being punished adequately for her horrid crimes.[9,10]

Danger signs
Munchausen syndrome

Pattern of crime
Administered high doses of insulin
and other drugs to patients

Number of victims
Four died; others were severely impaired

Chapter 4

CULT KILLERS AND RELIGIOUS-BELIEF KILLERS

Some serial killers get into black magic, satanic worship, or have a perverted view of religion. They may believe that killing is the only way to please the gods. They may have a grandiose view of who they are and what they can achieve. They may take advantage of others to do their bidding. They usually do not feel guilty for what they are doing because they feel they are doing the right thing according to their distorted view of the world.

Clementine Barnabet

Born: 1894

Profession: High Priestess of The Church of the Sacrifice

Motive: Vision, gain

Date of capture: November 27, 1911

Date of death: Unknown

Not much is known about the early life of Clementine Barnabet, who lived in Lafayette, Louisiana. At this time in the South, after the Civil War and the end of slavery, life was still hard for African Americans. The *El Paso Herald,* which reported on Barnabet's story in 1912, wrote that at this time "the life of a negro is held rather cheap." Barnabet was no doubt living in poverty. In an article in *Psychology Today* about Barnabet, psychologist Joni E. Johnston wrote, "Undoubtedly, there was a pervasive sense of injustice, hopelessness, and lack of control." Many in Louisiana eked out livings as rice pickers.

Young Clementine, who was also part Creole, became involved in The Church of the Sacrifice, which upheld a perverted belief that riches and immortality could be gained through human sacrifice. They may have also believed in killing off those who they believed were not following messages from God.

Clementine's church and the extent of its horrible deeds started to come to the attention of the public one day in February 1911.

This illustration from a Parisian journal depicts Clementine Barnabet performing a human sacrifice during a voodoo ceremony. Barnabet's church, The Church of the Sacrifice, taught that human sacrifice could

On that morning, Lezime Felix went to visit his sister Mimi and her family. When he arrived at 7 AM that day, he found a grotesque scene. Mimi, her husband, and their three-year-old son had been murdered—struck in the head with an axe. Their eleven-month-old baby was lifeless in the cradle with her head crushed. The murderer had apparently positioned the corpses of the mother and father in a kneeling position before the cradle of their dead baby, as if they were in prayer. The police who came to the scene said the crime resembled two previous murder scenes where African American families had been killed, which led the police to believe it was the work of the same terrible monster. Two months before this murder, a mother, father, and child were killed in a similar manner, and about a year and a half before, a family of four was murdered.

The police did not have a suspect for a while, in part because of the murder scenes—many of the victims had been chopped into small, unrecognizable bits, which left few clues for investigators. But in the fall of 1911, Barnabet's father Raymond was arrested and convicted for the murder of Mimi's family. Then, on November 26, 1911, it happened again. Norbert Randall, his wife, his three children, and a nephew were all murdered with an axe. When the police investigated, they saw Barnabet standing outside the house laughing. She was living within a block of the Randall family. Police escorted her to her home, where they found clothes with blood and brains on them. She was arrested on November 27, and at her hearing two days later, she confessed. Laughing and screaming, Barnabet told the court that the families had to be killed because they were not obeying orders from The Church of the Sacrifice. She revealed that she was the high priestess of the church, and murdering people was a means for her and other followers to live forever. She is quoted as saying, "We weren't afraid of being arrested because I carried a 'voodoo,' which protected us from all punishment." In her trial, she identified other church members who participated in the slaughter, which she led. The group as a whole claimed to have killed forty people. On October 25, 1912, Barnabet was sentenced to life in prison. Barnabet is widely regarded as the first African American serial killer. [1,2]

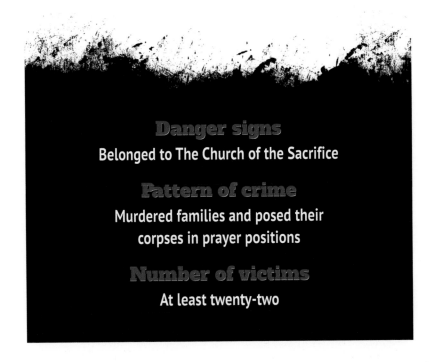

Danger signs
Belonged to The Church of the Sacrifice

Pattern of crime
Murdered families and posed their corpses in prayer positions

Number of victims
At least twenty-two

Leonarda Cianciulli
aka *"The Soap Maker of Correggio"*

Born: November 14, 1893
Profession: Mother, homemaker, shop owner
Motive: Delusion to keep her children alive
Date of capture: Fall 1940
Date of death: October 15, 1970

n Italy, Leonarda Cianciulli was born under a horribly dark cloud. Conceived by rape, the young girl was hated by her mother. Although her sadness drove her to attempt suicide twice, she forged on and met Rafaelle Pansardi, a registry office clerk. They fell in love and were married in 1914, when she was twenty-one. She led a quiet life for many years, but she had serious challenges with having children. Of her seventeen pregnancies, Cianciulli miscarried three and lost ten at young ages. Four of her children lived, and she felt compelled to fiercely protect them. Years earlier, a gypsy woman told her that her children would die, and she felt this prediction was coming true.

When Cianciulli's home in Alta Irpinia, Italy, was destroyed by an earthquake in 1930, the family moved to Correggio in Northern Italy. Despite living with a fear of losing her remaining offspring, Cianciulli became a nice, quiet, respected shop owner who had a fondness for

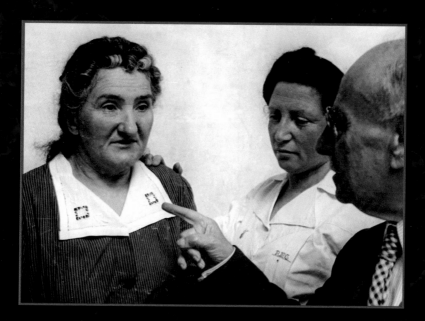

Leonarda Cianciulli is interviewed by psychiatrist and criminologist Fillipo Saporito. Cianciulli murdered her friends and used their bodies to make soaps and pastries.

That all changed in 1939, when her eldest son, Giuseppe, was drafted into the Italian Army as Benito Mussolini prepared for the start of World War II. She would do anything to prevent the gypsy's prediction from coming true and decided that the only way to keep her child safe was through human sacrifice. She had a bizarre notion that if she gave someone else's life, she would protect her child's life. She had four children, so she planned on four murders.

She decided that some of her lonely middle-aged friends would make perfect victims. Her first was Faustina Setti. Cianciulli

When her son joined Benito Mussolini's army prior to World War II, Cianciulli became worried. Plagued by the irrational fear that all her children would be taken from her, she murdered others as sacrifices to take the place of her children.

convinced her friend that she had found her a husband in a faraway town. She arranged for Setti to plan a trip to meet the husband and told her friend that she should write a few letters and postcards in advance saying that she was OK. Setti could send them to her family upon arrival. When Setti stopped to say goodbye to Cianciulli, she killed Setti with an axe. In a closet, she hacked the body into nine parts. What she did with the body is what makes the tale most horrendous and stomach-churning. Cianciulli said in her testimony:

> *I threw the pieces into a pot, added seven kilos [fifteen pounds] of caustic soda, which I had bought to make soap, and stirred the whole mixture until the pieces dissolved in a thick, dark mush that I poured into several buckets and emptied in a nearby septic tank. As for the blood in the basin, I waited until it had coagulated, dried it in the oven, ground it and mixed it with flour, sugar, chocolate, milk and eggs, as well as a bit of margarine, kneading all the ingredients together. I made lots of crunchy tea cakes and served them to the ladies who came to visit, though Giuseppe and I also ate them.*

This first plan worked so well that she used it again on her friend Francesca Soavi—this time telling her victim about a great job in another city. When Soavi stopped in to say goodbye on September 5, 1939, she wound up as soap and tea cakes, as well. Her final victim, Virginia Caccioppo, also wound up in a pot on September 30 of that year. To quote Cianciulli:

> *Her flesh was fat and white, when it had melted I added a bottle of cologne, and after a long time on the boil I was able to make some most acceptable creamy soap. I gave bars to*

neighbors and acquaintances. The cakes, too, were better: that woman was really sweet.

Virginia's sister-in-law became suspicious of her disappearance. When the police went to Cianciulli's house to investigate, she confessed to killing her friends. She was sentenced to thirty years in prison and three years in a criminal asylum. She died after spending thirty years imprisoned.[3,4]

Danger signs

Lost many children

Pattern of crime

Murdered friends as sacrifices

Number of victims

Three

Magdalena Solis
aka "The High Priestess of Blood"

Born: **Between 1930 and 1940**
Profession: **Prostitute**
Motive: **Power and gain**
Date of capture: **May 31, 1963**
Date of death: **Unknown**

Magdalena Solis was born into a poor family and supported herself through prostitution from a young age. It's likely she would have remained in obscurity if she hadn't met two brothers when she was in her twenties. Santos and Cayetano Hernandez were siblings and petty thieves. They weren't interested in killing; they only wanted to get money. In late 1962 and early 1963, they started scamming poor people in the small town of Yerba Buena, Mexico. Although these townfolk were poor, the brothers thought they could trick them out of their money. Because the townspeople were uneducated and had some knowledge of ancient Incan religion, the brothers came into town and told them that they were the prophets and priests of the ancient Incan gods. They promised the naïve people that they would have prosperity if they devoted their lives to them. Although the Inca were an ancient people from Peru and other areas in South America, the gullible people of Yerba Buena bought the story.

The Inca were known to sacrifice children to the gods to promote a healthy harvest and the working of the sun

Human sacrifice was an offering to the gods. The brothers told the villagers that they needed their money, personal belongings, sexual favors, and unquestioning loyalty, as well. In exchange, villagers would have to come to them in nearby caves, which the brothers called their temples. People basically became their slaves and fulfilled the brothers' fantasies, which they called religious rituals. Surprisingly, the people seemed willing to endure degrading treatment because they were promised riches from the gods in return. They even told the people they would see the gods.

After three months, however, the townspeople grew skeptical and disenchanted. No gods were appearing in any form. The brothers were growing accustomed to receiving anything they wanted from these people. To appease growing doubt among their followers, they hatched a new plan. They hired the prostitute Solis and her brother to dress as gods. In a sudden burst of smoke, they appeared before the people and told them they were the reincarnation of gods. Magdalena was especially convincing because she soon believed that she was a goddess. The people were convinced for a while, but two villagers soon grew disillusioned. When they tried to leave, they were brought before the Goddess Solis. She condemned the deserters to death.

The other villagers were horrified as they watched their friends being lynched, but they now feared Solis and would do as she said. Her killings became more violent and ritualistic. If she found a dissenter, he or she might be brutally beaten and cut by others in the cult. Then, while still alive, the victim would be bled. Solis would collect the human blood and sometimes mix it with chicken blood. She and the priests—her brother Eleazor Solis and the Hernandez brothers—would drink the blood and share it with cult members,

Born hustlers, Magdalena Solis and her brother tricked unsuspecting villagers into making sacrifices to ancient Incan gods. These included money, possessions, and even their lives.

as well. They claimed it would give them supernatural powers. Cult members would also sacrifice animals and get high on peyote and marijuana.

Solis veered from the original Incan script. She was convinced that she was the Aztec goddess Coatlicue, mother of the sun, stars, and moon. To stay young and live forever, she demanded more human blood. At least four people were sacrificed over the course of six weeks in 1963. Victims were butchered and their hearts removed. One spring night, a fourteen-year-old boy, Sebastian Guerrero, saw lights in the caves. He snuck up to where the cult was living and saw a person being beaten, burned, and hacked with a machete. He saw people drinking human blood. Fearing for his own life and wanting to save the others, he ran to the police in the nearby town of Villa Gran. The police didn't believe Guerrero's story, but to be nice, one officer, Luis Martinez, agreed to accompany the boy back to the scene of the crime. When the pair did not return, the police suspected foul play and sent a team of officers and soldiers from the Mexican Army to the caves in Yerba Buena. As they approached, gunfire broke out. During the intense shootout, a few cult members died, including Santos Hernandez.

Authorities captured Magdalena and her brother on May 31, 1963. As they combed through the caves, police found the bodies of Guerrero and Martinez. The officer's heart had been torn from his chest. They also discovered the dismembered bodies of six others. Magdalena and Eleazar Solis were tried for the murders of Guerrero and Martinez and sentenced to fifty years in prison. There have been no reports of Magdalena since that time. However, if she were alive, she may have been freed from prison in 2013.[5,6]

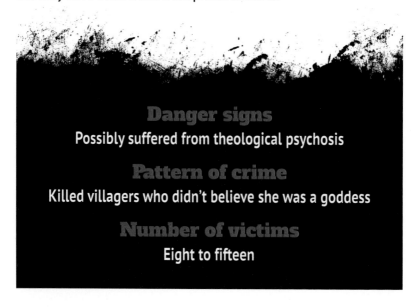

Danger signs
Possibly suffered from theological psychosis

Pattern of crime
Killed villagers who didn't believe she was a goddess

Number of victims
Eight to fifteen

Chapter 5

BLACK WIDOWS

So-called black widow killers are women who target romantic partners, relatives, and close friends. Like their arachnid namesake, they lure in unsuspecting victims then kill them when they are most vulnerable. They may kill for monetary gain, in the form of life insurance or an inheritance for example, or simply to be free of someone who is troubling them.

Belle Gunness
aka "Hell's Belle"

Born: **November 11, 1859**

Profession: **Farm girl, servant, housewife**

Motive: **Gain**

Date of capture: **Never captured**

Date of death: **Possibly April 28, 1908, but cannot be confirmed**

Born the youngest of eight children on a farm in Norway, Belle Gunness became pregnant at age seventeen. By some accounts, her father was so angry at her that he beat her, which caused her to miscarry. After the beating and losing her baby, Belle's personality seemed to change. Shortly after this episode, the baby's father also died, and some suspect he might have been killed by Belle. In another version of her early years, Belle was pregnant but beaten by a man who saw her at a country dance. That man died of stomach cancer soon afterward, but some believe it was the work of Belle. After saving up money by working on a farm, Belle sailed to America in 1881 to be with her sister and find her fortune there.

In Chicago, she met the man of her dreams, Mads Ditlev Anton Sorenson. They opened a confectionary store together and had four children. A census report shows they may have had a foster child living with them, as well. Business was not as strong as they hoped.

Belle Gunness is pictured with her children. From left: Lucy, age five; Myrtle, age seven; and Philip, age two. Gunness benefitted from insurance policy claims following the deaths of her husbands and some of her children.

Then, a year after opening, the store caught fire, but the Sorensons were able to collect on an insurance policy. Some claim that this taught Belle how to make money cashing in on insurance policies. During the next few years, two of her children died. The doctor said they had acute colitis, a disease that has symptoms similar to poisoning. No one doubted the prognosis, and Belle collected on two sizable life insurance policies she had taken out on her children.

Then, in 1900, Belle's husband Mads died conveniently on the one day when two life insurance policies on him overlapped. The doctor said his heart gave out, but some believe Belle may have slipped him strychnine on just the right day to collect double on the insurance. Her payout was the equivalent of about $217,000 by today's money value. The heartbroken Belle took some of her new fortune and bought property in Indiana. Soon after, a fire destroyed much of her new purchase, and again Belle collected on the insurance.

Seeking solace from all her tragedies, she met a man who had also lost his spouse. The widower, Peter Gunness, had two daughters from his marriage and could sympathize with Belle's situation. They wed on April 1, 1902. One of Peter's daughters was just an infant, and she mysteriously died one day under Belle's care. Misfortune seemed to follow Belle everywhere, but no one suspected that she was the cause. Less than a year since they married, in December 1902, Peter died in a freak accident. Belle said that a sausage-grinding machine accidentally fell from a high shelf and hit him on the head. She raked in a small fortune again from insurance. The remaining Gunness daughter must have been nervous, but fortunately her uncle swept in and took her away to live with him.

Belle may have steered any suspicion away from her with her sobs of grief and telling people she was pregnant with their first child. She gave birth to Phillip in May of 1903, and he joined the three remaining daughters of the family.

Belle then began to advertise for suitors. She was basically looking for men with some wealth who would want to "join fortunes." She had many replies, and most of these men disappeared. Many would give her a bit of money to demonstrate their wealth. Once she had a portion of their funds, they would vanish forever. Jennie, her foster daughter, supposedly told a classmate that her mother had killed Peter. Jennie was never seen again after 1906. Belle told friends that Jennie was off at school in Los Angeles.

Men came and went at a steady clip, ending with one unfortunate Andrew Helgelein. When he disappeared, his brother Asle thought something was not right. He contacted Belle, who told him that maybe Andrew had gone to Norway. Helgelein said he was determined to search for his brother. It's thought that with Asle coming to hunt for him, Belle felt she would be discovered. She had a trusted handyman who had helped her carry out many of her murders. She fired her handyman and drew up a will and testament. In this final note, she wrote that she feared for her life because her handyman was jealous of her suitors. After completing this document, her house mysteriously burned to the ground on April 28, 1908.

Investigators at the burning house immediately found the bodies of her three remaining children. There was also a decapitated woman's body, which was at first thought to be Belle herself. Without the head though, it was difficult to prove. The ex-handyman was arrested for murder and arson. His guilt made sense, especially

Police investigate the remains of Belle Gunness's home, where they found evidence of her grisly murders. Gunness's whereabouts became an unsolved mystery.

considering what Belle had written. But Asle told police that he thought Belle had been murdering men. The authorities did not believe him. Asle went himself to talk to the most recent handyman on the property. When he asked if there were ever any holes dug on the property, the new handyman took him to a spot near the hog pen. Asle grabbed a shovel and started digging. He pulled out four sacks. Inside, he found parts of his brother's chopped-up body. When the police arrived and dug further, they found the remains of forty-two people, including Belle's foster daughter, Jennie.

Meanwhile, the original handyman told police about his role in helping Belle Gunness kill all the missing men. He said he helped chop them up and either buried the parts or fed pieces to the pigs. While Gunness's dentures were found in the fire along with the headless woman, many doubted that Gunness really died in the fire. No definitive proof was ever found, and in fact, she had withdrawn most of her money from the bank the day before the blaze. Years after, people said they saw her in and around Chicago, but the fate of the black widow was never confirmed. She became known to some as the female Bluebeard, who in folktales had killed all his wives.[1,2]

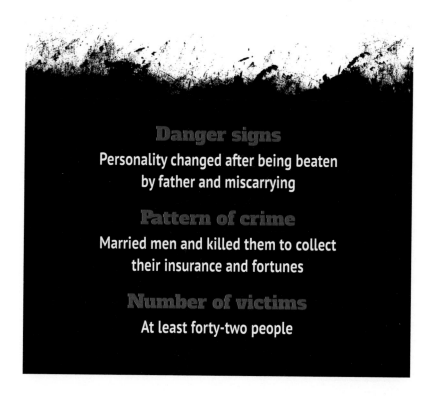

Danger signs

Personality changed after being beaten by father and miscarrying

Pattern of crime

Married men and killed them to collect their insurance and fortunes

Number of victims

At least forty-two people

Nannie Doss
aka "The Giggling Nanny"

Born: **November 4, 1905**
Profession: **Menial laborer and housewife**
Motive: **Gain**
Date of capture: **October 1954**
Date of death: **June 2, 1965 (in prison)**

When Nannie Doss was seven years old, she had an accident that she felt changed her forever. She was on a train trip in Alabama when the train abruptly stopped. Doss jolted forward and slammed her head hard into the seat in front of her. After that accident, Doss said she had pains and blackouts for months and headaches for the rest of her life. On top of this brain injury, Doss also had a traumatic childhood.

Born Nancy Hazle in Blue Mountain, Alabama, Doss had a strict and angry father. Nannie was her nickname, and she was later known as Doss from her last marriage. Because Doss often worked on the family farm with her four siblings, she missed a lot of school and was never a good student. She only completed the sixth grade. Her father forbade Doss from wearing makeup, attending dances, and going to social events. He wanted to prevent her from being molested by men but apparently it happened anyway on several occasions. Although she was not a strong reader, she enjoyed losing herself in romance magazines and thinking of falling in love in the future.

Nannie Doss served only ten years of her life sentence for murdering loved ones and collecting life insurance on her victims.

At sixteen, she got a job at a linen thread factory, where she met Charlie Braggs. They were soon married and had four daughters in quick succession. Their relationship became tumultuous, with Charlie drinking and each accusing the other of infidelity. In the beginning of 1927, six years after their marriage, two of their daughters had convulsions and died suddenly a few months apart. They had seemed healthy, so their deaths were a mystery. Braggs did not trust Nannie after this, so he left and took the older daughter, Melvina, with him. For some reason, he left behind his youngest daughter and his mother to live with Nannie. When he returned, his mother had died. Nannie then took custody of both remaining children, and Braggs left for good. They were soon officially divorced. She returned to reading romance magazines and she began corresponding with men in the lonely hearts column.

Robert Franklin "Frank" Harrelson was particularly smitten with Nannie. He sent her poetry, and she sent him a cake. They married in 1929, and the couple and Doss's two daughters all moved in together in Jacksonville. Although Harrelson turned out to be an alcoholic with a criminal record, their marriage lasted sixteen years until his death. When Melvina became a young woman in the early 1940s, she got married and became pregnant. She gave birth to Robert Lee Haynes and had a daughter two years later. When her daughter Melvina was giving birth, Doss was there to help. The doctors told her Melvina had a healthy girl, but soon after Doss held the newborn, it died. Doctors could not explain what happened.

Melvina was groggy from an exhausting labor but she noticed her mother holding a hatpin. At the time, she couldn't believe her mother would do such a thing, but later she suspected her mother pushed the pin into the baby's head.

Some time later, Melvina gave birth to a healthy baby boy. A short time after, Melvina went to visit her father and left young Robert in his grandmother's care. When Melvina returned from the trip, she found the boy had died from asphyxiation. With all these mysterious deaths surrounding Doss, you would think all who knew her would have fled, but they seemed to give her the benefit of the doubt—even though she collected a $500 life insurance claim on young Robert.

After sixteen years of marriage, her husband, Frank, was drinking heavily and becoming more abusive. While drunk, he would sexually force himself on Doss. Doss had enough. When she discovered his hidden stash of corn whiskey, she spiked it with rat poison, and Harrelson died in great pain that evening. Bodies were piling up around Doss, but still no one seemed inclined to blame happy Nannie.

Doss went back to the lonely hearts column and met a new man. She married Arlie Lanning, and they settled in a new town, Lexington, North Carolina. In a way, Lanning was a repeat of Harrelson—an alcoholic and a womanizer. But his bad habits didn't last long after meeting Nannie. He died in his sleep of apparent heart failure. Much of the town showed up at his funeral to give support to Doss. Arlie's family home was inherited by Lanning's sister. It mysteriously burned down after his death, and Doss collected an insurance payout on the home. Shortly thereafter, Arlie's mother died in her sleep. Then Nannie went to stay with her sister Dorie. Dorie soon took ill, and Nannie took care of her right up until she died. Doss now seemed to have the killing pattern down to an art.

She returned to the lonely hearts column and again married. She moved to Emporia, Kansas. In the beginning of 1953, Nannie's

Doss posed for this photograph with two unidentified people beside the casket of her third husband, Arlie Lanning. Police discovered at least one hundred similar pictures of Doss at funerals.

mother came to live with her and her fourth husband, Richard Morton. Within months of each other, her mother and Richard were both dead. Doss kept moving. This time she went to Tulsa, Oklahoma, and married the churchgoing Samuel Doss. He disapproved of all her romance magazines, and a short time into the marriage, he was rushed to the hospital with severe digestive tract pains. The hospital declared it an infection. On October 5, 1954, the night after the hospital released Samuel back into Nannie's care, he died.

This time, the sudden death drew the suspicion of the attending doctor. He ordered an autopsy and found that the cause of death was arsenic poisoning. Nannie was immediately arrested. As they traced back Nannie's history, investigators found the string of bodies she had left behind. When confronted with accusations of murder, Nannie would respond cheerfully that her conscience was clear. She would deny previous marriages at first, but then giggling, she would admit that she was caught in a lie. After bodies were exhumed and arsenic was found in many of them, she cheerfully confessed to killing eight—some through poisoning and some through smothering. She said she killed her husbands mostly out of marital boredom. She dreamed of finding the ideal husband, as described in her favorite romance magazines. As she was confessing to murders, she would say little anecdotal asides that added color to her testimony, like, "He sure did like stewed prunes." She joked and laughed with the press about her dead husbands and seemed to be getting a real hoot from all the attention that came with her arrest. The press dubbed her the Giggling Nanny, the Giggling Granny, and the Jolly Black Widow.

On May 18, 1955, she was sentenced to life in prison, and she went merrily to jail. She died in prison at age fifty-nine from leukemia.[3,4]

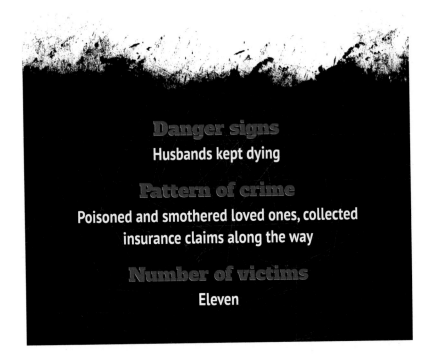

Danger signs

Husbands kept dying

Pattern of crime

Poisoned and smothered loved ones, collected insurance claims along the way

Number of victims

Eleven

Velma Barfield
aka "The Death Row Granny"

Born: October 23, 1932
Profession: Caretaker for the elderly
Motive: Gain
Date of capture: Unknown
Date of death: November 2, 1984 (executed)

Margie Velma Bullard was the oldest girl in a family of nine in South Carolina. Velma Barfield, as she would later be known, claimed she was raped and beaten by her father when she was a young girl. To try to escape this life and build a better one for herself, she married Thomas Burke when she was just seventeen. They had two children and Barfield said she was happy for a few years. Then, after her children were born, she had a hysterectomy and became addicted to tranquilizers, sleeping pills, antidepressants, and barbiturates that helped relieve pain from the operation. Her husband suffered injuries in a car crash that left him unable to work. When he turned to drinking, the couple argued more and more. On April 4, 1969, Barfield and the children left Thomas passed out drunk in the house. When they returned, they found the house on fire and Thomas dead inside. The house was not completely destroyed, but within months another mysterious fire consumed the rest of the home, and Barfield collected

A year after her husband's death, Velma married a widower, Jennings Barfield. Within a year of their first wedding anniversary, Jennings was dead from a heart condition. Velma was still taking drugs as she saw fit and was hospitalized four times with overdose symptoms. Still, she was considered a respectable widow and taught regular Sunday school classes at her church. Running short on money in 1974, she forged her mother's name to a loan application for $1,000. Then she worried that her aged mother might catch on to her scheme, so she fed her a lethal dose of insecticide. The doctors, however, said her old mother died from natural causes.

In 1976, Barfield gained employment working as a caretaker for the elderly. Hired by eighty-four-year-old Dollie Edwards, Barfield tended to Dollie's ninety-four-year-old husband, Montgomery Edwards, who was bedridden. She got along with the couple for a while and enjoyed living in their comfortable home. A year later, however, Barfield began to bicker with Dollie. In January 1977, Montgomery Edwards died from what appeared to be natural causes from old age. Barfield continued to help Dollie, but one month after Montgomery died, Dollie fell horribly ill with vomiting and diarrhea. She was taken to the hospital, treated, and released the same day. The very next day, however, she took a turn for the worse. She was rushed back to the hospital, where she died. Later, it was found that Barfield poisoned both, although no clear motive could be determined.

Velma Barfield moved on to find work tending to an eighty-year-old farmer, John Lee, and his seventy-six-year-old wife. Lee had broken his leg. Barfield forged a check for $50 in Lee's name. Worried she'd be found out, she slowly poisoned him over several

At age forty-six, Barfield went to work at a rest home and met Stuart Taylor, a fifty-six–year-old widower and tobacco farmer. She started to forge checks under his name to pay for her drug addiction. Because she feared being discovered, she began dosing his beer and tea with rat poison. As Taylor became ill, she nursed him with great attention and compassion. Even Taylor's children were moved by Barfield's care and devotion. Soon, Taylor had to be taken to the hospital, where he died. This time, however, Barfield was found out. An autopsy revealed large amounts of arsenic in Taylor's body. Barfield was arrested on May 13, 1978, and confessed to all her murders. She was sentenced to death. While on death row, she was described in *People* magazine as "a plump, hazel-eyed grandmother who reads her Bible daily, crochets dolls for her grandchildren and speaks in a soft, meek drawl." Velma Barfield was executed by lethal injection on November 2, 1984.[5,6]

Danger signs
Painkiller addiction made her desperate for money
Pattern of crime

Chapter 6

PARTNERSHIP KILLERS

As the name implies, serial killers known as partnership killers do not work alone but partner up with an accomplice—usually a boyfriend or husband. While some may seem to have been coerced into committing repulsive deeds, others are attracted to the sadistic behavior—the killings often have a sexual nature—and the appreciation they receive from their disturbed partner. In fact, there is a specific word for this attraction. Hybristophilia is an attraction to partners who have committed an outrageous crime, such as rape, murder, or armed robbery.[1]

Myra Hindley

aka "The Moors Murderer" and
"The Most Evil Woman in Britain"

Born: July 23, 1942
Profession: Clerk and typist
Motive: Lust
Date of capture: October 11, 1965
Date of death: November 16, 2002 (in prison)

The first child of Nellie Hettie and Bob Hindley, Myra Hindley was raised near Manchester, England. Bob Hindley was away serving with the parachute regiment during the first three years of Myra's life, and when he returned, he had trouble getting back into civilian life. When Myra's parents had a second child, Maureen, they felt overwhelmed and sent Myra to live with her grandmother, who then raised her.

Some say the absence of Myra's father during her formative years may have played a role in how she developed psychologically. Bob Hindley drank heavily and was abusive to his wife, Nellie. He taught Myra that it was important to stand up to others and fight, and little Myra gained a reputation as a street fighter. She defended her little sister, Maureen, and her friend Pauline. She was always considered mature for her age, and parents loved to hire her as a babysitter. In

The culture of violence in which Myra Hindley was raised affected her perception of acceptable behavior. When she took judo lessons as a teen, she had trouble finding partners because she was too rough.

At age fifteen, Myra became good friends with thirteen-year-old Michael Higgins, who was frail by comparison. One day, he drowned while swimming. Myra was devastated and thought she could have saved him if she had been there. She was so distraught over Michael's death that she had severe bouts of depression and hysteria. Her grades plummeted, and she eventually dropped out of school. She worked various clerk jobs and met a boy she thought she might marry. But when Hindley thought of settling down, she found the idea boring. She wanted excitement.

She looked into joining the military, but when she met Ian Brady, she was swept away. He was quiet and sullen with a bad boy image and a criminal record. Here was the excitement she was looking for. Brady was obsessed with Nazis and eager to talk to Hindley about all his thoughts. Hindley was an attentive, besotted audience. She dyed her hair blond to look more German. He told her there was no God, and she believed all he said. They read about the Marquis de Sade, from whose name the word "sadism" originates, and they read Hitler's *Mein Kampf* and Dostoyevsky's *Crime and Punishment*, about the murderer Rashkolnikov, who kills simply because he desperately needs to do something. They went to X-rated films, bought guns, and took up the hobby of photography. Brady took risqué photos of Hindley. She wrote in her diary, "He is cruel and selfish and I love him."

In July 1963, Brady began talking to Hindley about the case of Leopold and Loeb, two well-to-do young men from Chicago. They wanted to carry out the perfect murder. On July 12, 1964, Brady and Hindley set out to kill someone just to see what it would be like. Hindley convinced her sister's friend, the now sixteen-year-old Pauline Reade, to help her search for a glove she said she had lost

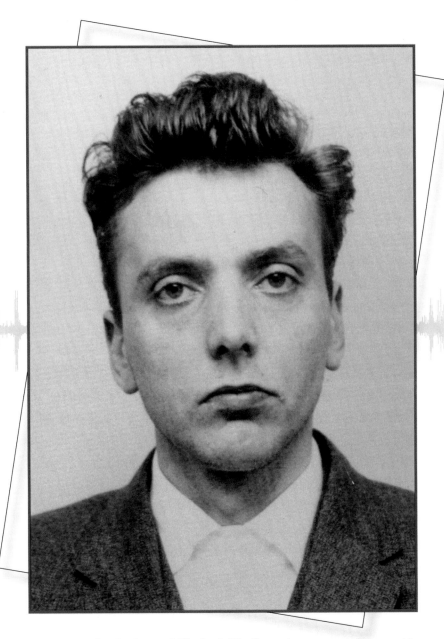

Meeting Ian Brady changed Hindley's life. Soon the two were inseparable and murdering for the fun of it.

on the moors. Brady accompanied them. Once at the moors, Brady beat Pauline, raped her, and slit her throat. The couple buried her on the moors and drove home. Once they had killed, they wanted to kill again. On November 23, 1963, they abducted twelve-year-old John McKilbride. Brady again sexually assaulted him, killed him, and buried him on the moors. Thousands volunteered in the search for the missing boy. On June 16, 1964, the same fate befell twelve-year-old Keith Bennett.

Their next murder was perhaps their most depraved killing. It happened the day after Christmas 1964. The couple kidnapped

Police searched the Manchester, England, house where Ian Brady murdered Edward Evans. Brady and Hindley were done in when they included an accomplice in their evil deeds.

ten-year-old Lesley Ann Downey. They bound her, beat her, and took photos of her naked and tied up. They also made a sound tape recording of her begging for her life. On the tape, Hindley and Brady can both be heard threatening the girl.

Authorities conducted a huge search, but they could not find any of the missing children. By now, the couple must have thought they were unstoppable. Their downfall came when Brady had become friendly with Hindley's brother-in-law, seventeen-year-old David Smith. Brady wanted to introduce Smith to the world of killing. Brady met a teenager named Edward Evans and invited him over to have some wine with him and Hindley. He also invited Smith. As they were enjoying wine, Brady unexpectedly went for an axe and bludgeoned Evans to death in front of Smith. Smith was shocked, but he helped Brady wrap up the body in plastic to be disposed of the next day. He calmly left but then contacted authorities. Smith's tipoff to the police led to Hindley and Brady's arrest and put an end to their killing spree. Police found Brady's notebook, in which he had written, "Murder is a hobby and a supreme pleasure." They also found photos of the couple on the moors, smiling and posing on the graves where they buried their victims. Myra Hindley and Ian Brady were both sentenced to life in prison. Hindley died in prison, and Brady is still alive.[2,3,4]

Hindley lured ten-year-old Lesley Ann Downey from a fairground on Boxing Day. The couple brought her home, where they sexually assaulted and killed her. They buried the little girl's body on the Saddleworth Moor.

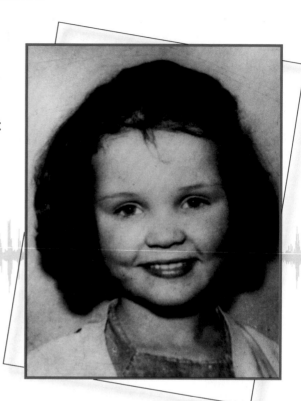

Danger signs
Need for excitement; pairing with Ian Brady

Pattern of crime
Tortured and killed young people for pleasure

Number of victims
Five

Rosemary West

aka "The Gloucester House of Horrors Murderer"

Born: **November 29, 1953**
Profession: **Prostitute**
Motive: **Lust, thrill**
Date of capture: **February 25, 1994**
Date of death: **Still alive in prison**

Born in Barnstaple, about four hours west of London, England, Rosemary Letts grew up to be a moody teenager. During her teen years, her parents divorced, and she did poorly in school. She moved in with her father, who would force himself on her sexually—something that Rosemary grew to accept and would continue throughout her young adult life.

Around this same time, teenage Rosemary met Fred West, who was twenty-seven years old and married to Rena Costello. West and Costello had two children. Like Rosemary, West also had grown up in an abusive, poor household. He had suffered a head injury in a motorcycle accident at age fifteen and had fits of rage thereafter. At age twenty, he was convicted of molesting a thirteen-year-old girl—it was certainly a sign of things to come. While married to Costello, West had a relationship with their nanny and impregnated and killed her. Along the way, he had worked as a butcher, and it seems

Fred and Rosemary West were a lethal combination. Together the couple sexually assaulted, tortured, murdered, and dismembered women, including their own daughters.

this work may have triggered West's obsession with corpses, blood, and dismemberment.

As Rosemary became involved with Fred, she found out about his interest in sadistic and masochistic acts such as bondage. Experts say she was not put off by his perverted sexual desires because her relationship with her father was based on abuse. By age sixteen, Rosemary was living with Fred and pregnant with his baby. They would have eight children total, although three were fathered by clients through Rosemary's work as a prostitute. They also lived with Fred's two children, Charmaine and Anne Marie. In 1971, Fred was jailed for theft. While away from home, nineteen-year-old Rosemary apparently lost her temper with Charmaine and killed her. She buried the girl in their yard. According to reports, Fred's first wife disappeared after dropping by to collect Charmaine. Years later, her murdered body was found.

Fred and Rosemary's behavior became increasingly depraved. Fred would have relations with his daughters while Rosemary watched. In 1973, they hired Caroline Roberts to be their nanny. They held her captive and sexually assaulted her. The couple was fined for indecent assault. But that didn't stop their behavior. The deranged couple imprisoned several women, tortured them, and sexually assaulted them. They then strangled or suffocated the women and dismembered their bodies.

Fred and Rosemary West carried on most of their murders for eight years—mostly with women who were not missed by family. From 1979 until 1987, the murders appeared to stop. But that year, Fred got upset with his daughter Heather and killed her. He dismembered her body and buried it in the yard with the others.

A forensics team digs up the garden at 25 Cromwell Street in Gloucester, England. The residence is one of two homes where the Wests buried remains of their murder victims.

Still, they might have gotten away with their depraved murders if they had not continued to sexually assault their children. When social workers heard of possible abuse in 1992, they went to investigate and heard the West children joking about how their sister Heather was buried under the patio. This was enough to order a search, which uncovered the extent of their crimes. All in all, there were twelve confirmed murders, and Rosemary was convicted of ten. Rosemary was found to play a crucial role in luring the women into their home and making them feel at ease. Fred may have done the actual killing, but Rosemary was instrumental and participated in torture and sexual acts. In the end, testimony from her children and a woman who escaped the Wests convinced the jury to find Rosemary guilty. Fred hanged himself in jail, and Rosemary is serving out a life prison sentence.[5,6]

Danger signs
Childhood abuse; took up with a sadistic husband

Pattern of crime
Lured young women home to torture and kill them

Number of victims
At least ten

Chapter 7

REVENGE KILLERS

Those serial killers classified as revenge killers may be seeking some sort of perceived justice for a wrong that was committed against them earlier in their lives. Aileen Wuornos led a life marked by abuse from men. Juana Barraza seemed to never forgive her mother for mistreatment when she was a child. These women may have had other motivations and mental problems that drove them to kill, but they appeared to have reasons to seek a type of perceived revenge, and their revenge took the form of murder.

Aileen Wuornos
aka "The Florida Highway Killer"

Born: **February 29, 1956**
Profession: **Highway prostitute**
Motive: **Revenge**
Date of capture: **January 1, 1991**
Date of death: **October 9, 2002 (executed)**

Growing up in Rochester, Michigan, Wuornos had an extremely troubled childhood. Her mother abandoned her as an infant, her father committed suicide following a child molestation conviction, her grandfather physically abused her and later committed suicide, and she had a sexual relationship with her brother at a young age. At age eleven, she began trading sexual favors for beer, cigarettes, and money. Her junior high school gave her mild tranquilizers to calm her. After being raped at fourteen and having her resulting child put up for adoption, she dropped out of school and began a difficult life as a prostitute.

At age twenty, however, it looked like Wuornos might settle down. While hitchhiking in Florida, she met the wealthy and retired sixty-nine-year-old Lewis Gratz Fell. Fell loved the idea of being with a beautiful young blonde. The two got married, but their relationship was short-lived. Wuornos took to getting drunk and getting in fights in local bars. When she hit her husband with his cane, he filed a restraining order on her, and they divorced soon after.

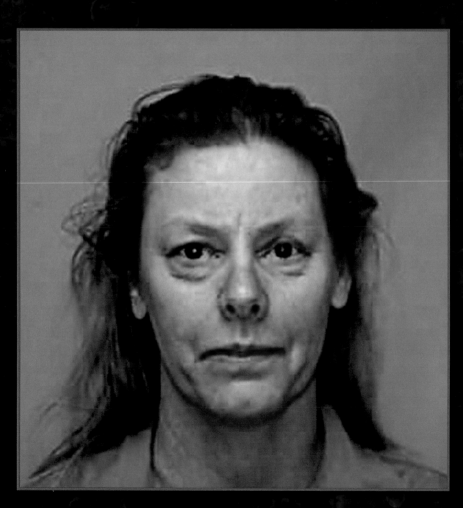

One of the most notorious female serial killers, Aileen Wuornos murdered at least seven men. Her early experiences as a victim of sexual abuse and rape may have fueled her desire to seek revenge on men.

Wuornos returned to her home state of Michigan and continued her drinking and fighting ways. She was charged with assault when she threw a cue ball at a bartender's head. In 1976, her brother died of esophageal cancer, and she collected $10,000 in life insurance. She went back to Florida, where the next several years were marked by a string of arrests, including armed robbery, passing forged checks, and grand theft auto. Along the way, she acquired a .22 caliber pistol. Around 1986, she met a hotel maid, Tyria Moore, in a gay bar in Daytona, and they started a romantic relationship. They lived together, and Wuornos supported them through prostitution.

For her first slaying, Wuornos flagged down video repair shop owner Richard Mallory. He turned out to be a convicted rapist. She robbed him and shot him to death with a .22 caliber pistol she kept in her purse. Wuornos said she killed him in self-defense. She later confessed to killing Mallory and six more middle-aged white men over the course of a year from 1989 to 1990. The men included a construction worker, a part-time rodeo worker, a sausage salesman, and a former chief of police—all of whom had solicited her for sex. While she claimed that Mallory tried to rape her, she said the others had not—although she told authorities that she killed them all in self-defense. Ultimately, she told the Florida State Supreme Court, "I'm one who seriously hates human life and would kill again."

Wuornos said that she only killed when a man gave her a problem, but her killings seemed to be triggered by some deep-seated hatred of men. James Alan Fox, a professor of criminal justice and coauthor of *Mass Murder: America's Growing Menace*, wrote that she had grown fed up with being dominated by men, and killing them was a way for her to gain control, power, and dominance. In addition, some mental health experts characterized her as having borderline personality disorder. This is defined as having "a pervasive pattern of instability of interpersonal relationships, self-image, and affects, and marked impulsivity," according to *The Diagnostic and Statistical Manual of Mental Disorders*.

When in jail, she was also found to be delusional and paranoid. She acted like a sociopath rather than a psychopath. She is an example of a disorganized killer—she appeared to be psychotic, and her murders were not planned but spontaneous. The judge in her case also found her to have antisocial personality disorder. She had violent outbursts her whole life.

The hearse carrying the body of convicted killer Aileen Wuornos leaves the Florida State Prison following her execution by lethal injection on October 9, 2002 in Starke, Florida. Wuornos, who was the first woman to be profiled by the FBI as a serial killer, was sentenced to death for killing six men along central Florida highways in 1989 and 1990.

She was deemed mentally fit to be executed and put to death by lethal injection on October 9, 2002. Documentary filmmaker Nick Broomfield interviewed Wuornos when she was in prison. She told him that her mind was being controlled by "sonic pressure" and she was going to be taken away by angels on a spaceship. Broomfield came to the conclusion that Wuornos was insane. Her last words before execution were, "Yes, I would just like to say I'm sailing with the rock, and I'll be back, like Independence Day with Jesus. June 6, like the movie. Big mother ship and all, I'll be back, I'll be back."[1,2,3,4]

Danger signs

Abusive childhood, including rape

Pattern of crime

Killed men who threatened her

Number of victims

At least seven

Juana Barraza

aka "The Old Lady Killer"

Born: December 27, 1958
Profession: Professional wrestler
Motive: Revenge
Date of capture: January 24, 2006
Date of death: Currently serving a life
sentence of 759 years

Born into poverty in Hidalgo, Mexico, to an alcoholic mother, Juana Barraza was reportedly given away at a young age to a man who sexually abused her. She became pregnant at age twelve. Barraza went on to have four children from three different fathers. While she supported her children through domestic work, street vending, and petty theft, she also wrestled in full Lucha Libre dress on the amateur wrestling circuit. She was known as La Dama del Silencio and engaged in epic fake battles in the ring. She wore an elaborate costume that made her look almost like a cartoon character.

From 2002 until 2006, a series of women over the age of sixty were killed in Mexico City. They were either bludgeoned or strangled to death with cables, scarves, or stockings. Witnesses reported seeing a large woman at the scenes of the crimes. Because of the violence inflicted on these women, investigators thought they were dealing with a man dressed as a woman, and they started interviewing Mexico City's transgender prostitutes.

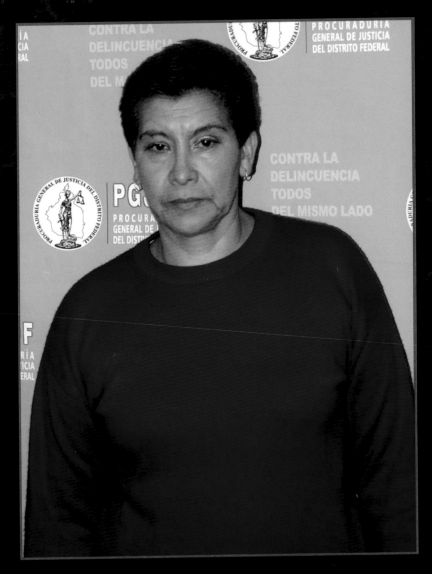

Juana Barraza targeted elderly women, gained their trust, and murdered them. Her actions may have been an attempt to combat the rage she felt against her own mother.

Adding to the bizarre nature of her case was the fact that Barraza performed as the Silent Lady. Barraza was obsessed with Lucha Libre, a form of professional wrestling in Mexico in which participants are masked.

On January 25, 2006, Barraza was nabbed as she fled a woman's home. Police found her carrying a stethoscope, social benefits papers, and a social worker's identification card. Apparently she would fake being a government employee to get into women's homes, and the stethoscope made for a handy strangling tool. Barraza also closely matched the police sketch of their suspect. From the evidence police acquired and a confession from Barraza, she was connected with at least eleven murders, but authorities suspected links to many murders going back to the 1990s. News reports at the time said she took symbolic trophies, such as ornaments or religious items from some of the old women's homes.[5,6]

During her trial, Barraza admitted to killing only one victim even though evidence connected her to at least ten. Nevertheless, she was found guilty on eleven counts of murder and sentenced to 759 years in prison for her deeds.

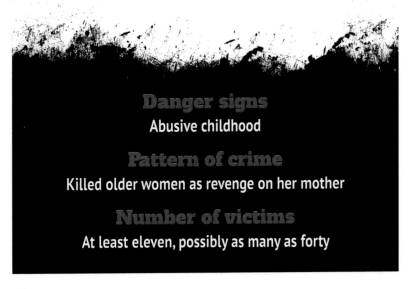

Danger signs
Abusive childhood

Pattern of crime
Killed older women as revenge on her mother

Number of victims
At least eleven, possibly as many as forty

CONCLUSION

Motivations behind serial killings are always complex. There is usually not one simple reason why a serial killer may be pushed to murder. While the number of women serial killers is far fewer than their male counterparts, there are nonetheless women who take this journey into darkness.

Psychologists and criminologists who have studied murder often come back to a basic question: Are serial killers born with a will to kill, or do they develop into killers because of experiences that shape their lives? Perhaps it is a combination of factors. Adrian Raine, a professor at the University of Pennsylvania, has studied this subject extensively. He is also the author of *The Anatomy of Violence: The Biological Roots of Crime*. From his years of research, Raine has found that while there are social and environmental factors that spur violent behavior, biology plays a huge role. People are either born that way or go through a physical trauma that causes brain dysfunction. Raine believes that research on the minds of serial killers is important because it can help identify those who may be inclined toward violent behavior. This research may also help rehabilitate murderers or those who may be prone to violence. Ultimately, the more we understand about serial killing, the more likely we will be to prevent it and stop unnecessary and brutal murders by both men and women.[1]

Psychopathy Quiz

Are You a Psychopath?

This quiz is designed to help give you some insight into people with psychopathic tendencies. While the quiz is not meant to diagnose psychopathy, it may also give you an idea about whether or not *you* have such tendencies.

Read each of the following statements and answer each honestly. Give yourself two points if the statement definitely describes you, one point if it somewhat describes you, and zero points if it doesn't describe you at all. Tally up the points to see where *you* sit on the psychopathy scale!

1. I'd rather be spontaneous than make plans.
2. I wouldn't have a problem cheating on a boyfriend or girlfriend if I knew I could get away with it.
3. I don't mind ditching plans to hang out with my friends if something better comes along—such as a chance to go out with a hot new guy or girl.
4. Seeing animals injured or in pain doesn't bother me.
5. I love excitement and danger.
6. I think it's OK to manipulate others so I can get ahead.
7. I'm a smooth talker—I can always get people to do what I want.
8. I'm great at making quick decisions.
9. I don't get it when movies or TV shows make people cry.
10. Most people just bring problems upon themselves, so why should I help them?

11. I'm rarely to blame when things go wrong—it's others who are incompetent, not me.

12. I have more talent in the tip of my little finger than most people will ever have.

13. I am able to make other people believe my lies.

14. I don't feel guilty when I make people feel bad.

15. I often borrow things and then lose or forget to return them.

16. I skip school or work more than most people I know.

17. I tend to blurt out exactly what's on my mind.

18. I often get into trouble because I lie a lot.

19. I skip school or often don't get my assignments done on time.

20. I think that crying is a sign of weakness.

If you scored 30–40 points, you have many psychopathic tendencies.

If you scored 20–39 points, you have some psychopathic tendencies.

If you scored 0–19 points, you have no psychopathic tendencies.

Chapter Notes

Introduction

1. Tom and Michael Philbin, *The Killer Book of True Crime: Incredible Stories, Facts and Trivia from the World of Murder and Mayhem* (Naperville, IL: Sourcebooks, 2007), p. 224.
2. Eric Hickey, *Serial Murderers and Their Victims* (Belmont, CA: Wadsworth Publishing, 2009), p. 6.
3. Deborah Schurman-Kauflin, "7 Steps for Working a Serial Female Serial Murder Case," *Psychology Today*, October 24, 2011, (https://www.psychologytoday.com/blog/disturbed/201110/7-steps-working-female-serial-murder-case).
4. Hickey, p. 312.
5. "Research—Serial Killers," Victims of Violence, (http://www.victimsofviolence.on.ca/rev2/index.php?option=com_content&task=view&id=362&Itemid=52).
6. Robert J. Morton, ed., "Serial Murder: Multi-Disciplinary Perspectives for Investigators," Federal Bureau of Investigation, (https://www.fbi.gov/stats-services/publications/serial-murder).
7. "Female Serial Killers," Serial Killers Defined, (http://twistedminds.creativescapism.com/serial-killers-introduction/kehler-typology/).
8. "Female Serial Killers," Psyed.org, (http://psyed.org/r/psd/pd/pdd/male_v_female_killers.html).
9. Meredith Galante, "There Are Two Types of Serial Killers and It's Easy to Tell Them Apart," *Business Insider,* April 12, 2012, (http://www.businessinsider.com/types-of-serial-killers-2012-4).
10. "Types of Serial Killers,." The Crime Museum, (http://www.crimemuseum.org/crime-library/types-of-serial-killers).
11. Scott A. Bonn, "How to Tell a Sociopath from a Psychopath," *Psychology Today,* January 22, 2014, (https://www.psychologytoday.com/blog/wicked-deeds/201401/how-tell-sociopath-psychopath).

Chapter 1: Sexual Predators and Thrill Killers

1. Richard Cavendish, "Death of Countess Elizabeth Bathory," History Today, August 8, 2014, (http://www.historytoday.com/richard-cavendish/death-countess-elizabeth-bathory).

2. "Elizabeth Bathory: The Blood Countess," Rejected Princesses, (http://www.rejectedprincesses.com/princesses/elisabeth-bathory).
3. "Elizabeth Bathory, The Blood Countess," Scandalous Women, (http://scandalouswoman.blogspot.com/2009/10/elizabeth-bathory-blood-countess.html).
4. "Marie Delphine Lalaurie," Murderpedia, (http://murderpedia.org/female.L/l/lalaurie-delphine.htm).
5. Erin Bass and Anne Wheeler, "The Real Madame Lalaurie & Other Legends From American Horror Story: Coven," *Deep South Magazine*, January 15, 2014, (http://deepsouthmag.com/2014/01/the-real-madame-lalaurie-other-legends-from-american-horror-story-coven/).
6. "History of Delphine Lalaurie," Nola.com, (http://www.nola.com/lalaurie/history/intro.html).
7. "French Child Care Provider, Jeanne Weber, Murdered 7 Children—1908," The Unknown History of Misandry, September 17, 2011, (http://unknownmisandry.blogspot.com/2011/11/french-child-care-provider-jeanne-weber.html).
8. "French Ogress Again Arrested," *The New York Times*, May 5, 1907, (http://query.nytimes.com/mem/archive-free/pdf?_).
9. Vikram Dodd, "Joanna Dennehy: Serial Killer Becomes First Woman Told by Judge to Die in Jail," *Guardian*, February 28, 2014, (http://www.theguardian.com/uk-news/2014/feb/28/joanna-dennehy-serial-killer-first-woman-die-in-jail).
10. Dominic Gover, "Joanna Dennehy: Inside the Mind of a Female Psychopath Serial Killer," *International Business Times*, February 13, 2014, (http://www.ibtimes.co.uk/joanna-dennehy-inside-mind-female-psychopath-serial-killer-1436317).
11. Steve Morris, "Murder Sprees Left Joanna Dennehy 'Stinking of Blood,'" *The Guardian*, February 12, 2014, (http://www.theguardian.com/uk-news/2014/feb/12/joanna-dennehy-murder-spree-jacobean-tragedy).

Chapter 2: Profit or Crime Killers

1. "Lavinia Fisher," Murderpedia, (http://www.murderpedia.org/female.F/f/fisher-lavinia.htm).

2. Kathy Weiser, "Lavinia Fisher,." Legends of America, Updated July 15, 2015, (http://www.legendsofamerica.com/sc-laviniafisher.html).

3. Oscar Ricket, "Hunting for the Vampire of Barcelona," *Vice,* January 28, 2014, (http://www.vice.com/read/the-vampire-of-barcelona-shadows-marc-pastor-enriqueta-marti).

4. "Enriqueta Marti Ripolles," Murderpedia, (http://murderpedia.org/female.M/m/marti-enriqueta.htm).

5. "Delfina and María de Jesús Gonzalez," Murderpedia, (http://murderpedia.org/female.G/g/gonzalez-sisters.htm).

6. Kehinde Ajayi, "Las Poquianchis: The Macabre Case That Shocked Mexico," Prezi, December 5, 2014, (https://prezi.com/q4_xs6uyfyvk/las-poquianchis-the-macabre-case-that-shocked-mexico/).

Chapter 3: Angels of Death

1. Sreeja VN. "'Angel Maker' Amelia Dyer Killed 400 Babies in 19th Century, Records Show," *International Business Times,* February 24, 2013, (http://www.ibtimes.com/angel-maker-amelia-dyer-killed-400-babies-19th-century-records-show-1101722).

2. "Amelia Elizabeth Dyer," Murderpedia, (http://murderpedia.org/female.D/d/dyer-amelia.htm).

3. "Maria Swanenburg, Dutch Serial Killer," November 11, 2010, (http://culture-society.todio.info/history/the-serial-killer-maria-swanenburg-696.html).

4. "Maria Swanenburg (Van der Linden), Dutch Serial Killer—1883," The Unknown History of Misandry, September 22, 2011, (http://unknownmisandry.blogspot.com/2011/09/maria-swanenburg-dutch-serial-killer.html).

5. "Jane Toppan," Murderpedia, (http://murderpedia.org/female.T/t/toppan-jane.htm).

6. Chelsea Lyle, "Jane Toppan, the Nightmare Nurse," Women Serial Killers, February 14, 2011, (http://womenserialkillers.blogspot.com/2011/02/jane-toppan-nightmare-nurse.html).

7. "Miyuki Ishikawa, "Japanese Childcare Provider & Serial Baby-Killer—1948," The Unknown History of Misandry, September 19, 2011, (http://unknownmisandry.blogspot.com/2011/09/miyuki-ishikawa-japanese-childcare.html).
8. "Miyuki Ishikawa," Murderpedia, (http://murderpedia.org/female.I/i/ishikawa-miyuki.htm).
9. "Beverly Gail Allitt," Murderpedia, (http://murderpedia.org/female.A/a/allitt-beverley.htm).
10. David Batty, "Serial Killer Nurse Allitt Must Serve 30 Years," *UK News,* December 6, 2007, (http://www.theguardian.com/uk/2007/dec/06/ukcrime.health).

Chapter 4: Cult Killers and Religious-Belief Killers

1. "Clementine Barnabet, Louisiana Serial Killer & Voodoo Priestess—1911," The Unknown History of Misandry, September 22, 2011, (http://unknownmisandry.blogspot.com/2011/09/clementine-barnabet-louisiana-serial.html).
2. Joni Johnston, "Female Cult Leaders Who Kill," *Psychology Today.* May 7, 2012, (https://www.psychologytoday.com/blog/the-human-equation/201205/female-cult-leaders-who-kill).
3. "Leonarda Cianciulli—The Soap Maker of Correggio," UndergroundHerald.com, April 19, 2015, (http://undergroundherald.com/2015/04/19/leonarda-cianciulli-the-soap-maker-of-correggio/).
4. "The Soap Maker: The Chilling Crimes of Italy's First Female Serial Killer," First to Know, August 28, 2015, (http://firsttoknow.com/the-soap-maker-the-chilling-crimes-of-italys-first-female-serial-killer/).
5. "Magdalena Solis: Cult Leader, Blood Drinker & Deadly Serial Killer," Crimefeed.com, March 13, 2015, (http://crimefeed.com/2015/03/sex-slaves-ritual-sacrifices-learn-magdalena-solis-became-high-priestess-blood/).
6. "Magdalena Solis, 'The High Priestess of Blood,' Mexican Serial Killer—1963," The Unknown History of Misandry, September 22, 2011, (http://unknownmisandry.blogspot.com/2011/09/magdalena-solis-high-priestess-of-blood.html).

Chapter 5: Black Widows

1. "Belle Gunness," Bio, (http://www.biography.com/people/belle-gunness-235416).
2. Mara Bovsun, "Belle Gunness, Queen of Black Widows, Murdered Dozens and Planted Victims around Farm," *Daily News*, November 30, 2014, (http://www.nydailynews.com/news/crime/queen-black-widows-murdered-dozens-farm-article-1.2028012).
3. Charles Montaldo, "Nannie Doss," About News, (http://crime.about.com/od/serial/a/Nannie-Doss.htm).
4. Cheryl Eddy, "The "Giggling Granny Serial Killer Who Smiled All the Way to Prison," True Crime, July 15, 2015, (http:// truecrime.io9.com/the-giggling-granny-serial-killer-who-smiled-all-the-1718086506).
5. Eric Levin, "Cunning Poisoner—or Redeemed Christian—Velma Barfield Draws Nearer to Her Day of Execution," *People*, October 29, 1984, (http://www.people.com/people/archive/article/0,,20089011,00.html).
6. "Velma Margie Barfield," ClarkProsecutor.org, (http://www.clarkprosecutor.org/html/death/US/barfield029.htm).

Chapter 6: Partnership Killers

1. Ryan Buxton, "Explaining Hybristophilia: Why Some People Are Sexually Attracted to Serial Killers," HuffPost Live, November 20, 2014, (http://www.huffingtonpost.com/2014/11/20/hybristophilia-serial-killers_n_6194386.html).
2. "The Horrific Truth about Evil Lovers Ian Brady and Myra Hindley," *Daily Star*, November 17, 2013, (http://www.dailystar.co.uk/real-life/351240/The-horrific-truth-about-evil-lovers-Ian-Brady-and-Myra-Hindley).
3. Nikki Murfitt, "Will This Photo Finally Lead Police to Keith Bennett's Grave? Chilling Image of Killer Brady Just 40 Miles from Where Moors Murders Detectives Have Searched for 50 Years," *Daily Mail*, June 15, 2013, (http://www.dailymail.co.uk/news/article-2342296/Moors-murders-Chilling-image-killer-Brady-just-40-miles-Moors-Murders-detectives-searched-50-years.html).

4. "Myra Hindley," Murderpedia, (http://murderpedia.org/female.H/h/hindley-myra.htm).

5. Jane Carter Woodrow,. "A Killer and a Sex Offender Drawn Together by Evil," Express, July 3, 2011, (http://www.express.co.uk/expressyourself/256432/A-killer-and-a-sex-offender-drawn-together-by-evil).

6. "Rosemary West, One of the Most Shocking Sadists in Female Serial Killer History—England, 1994," The Unknown History of Misandry, August 23, 2014, (http://unknownmisandry.blogspot.com/2014/08/rosemary-west-one-of-most-shocking.html).

Chapter 7: Revenge Killers

1. "Aileen Wuornos," Crime Investigation, (http://www.crimeandinvestigation.co.uk/crime-files/aileen-wuornos).

2. "The Case of Aileen Wuornos," Capital Punishment in Context, (http://www.capitalpunishmentincontext.org/cases/wuornos).

3. "Aileen Wuornos," Twisted Minds, (http://twistedminds.creativescapism.com/most-notorious/aileen-wuornos/).

4. Nancy Ramsey, "Social Outcast to Serial Killer," New York Times, January 14, 2004, (http://articles.sun-sentinel.com/2004-01-14/lifestyle/0401130265).

5. Jo Tuckman "Little Old Lady Killer Handed 759 years in a Mexican Prison," Guardian, April 1, 2008, (http://www.theguardian.com/world/2008/apr/02/mexico).

6. "Juana Barraza 'The Old Lady Killer,' Mexican Serial Killer—2006," The Unknown History of Misandry, September 22, 2011, (http://unknownmisandry.blogspot.com/2011/09/juana-barraza-old-lady-killer-mexican.html).

Conclusion

1. Adrian Raine, The Anatomy of Violence, New York: Vintage (2014).

Glossary

antisocial personality disorder—A chronic mental condition in which a person typically has no regard for right and wrong and often ignores the rights, wishes, and feelings of others.

arsenic—A metallic element that forms a number of poisonous compounds; used in insecticides and weed killers.

autopsy—A highly specialized surgical procedure that consists of a thorough examination of a corpse to determine the cause and manner of death and evaluate any disease or injury that may be present.

black magic—The use of magic and supernatural powers to achieve evil ends.

bludgeon—To beat someone repeatedly with a heavy object.

convulsions—Sudden violent, irregular movements of a limb or of the body caused by involuntary contraction of muscles and associated especially with brain disorders such as epilepsy, the presence of certain toxins in the blood, or fever in children.

corpse—A dead body.

criminologist—A professional who analyzes data to determine why a crime was committed and to find ways to predict, deter, and prevent further criminal behavior.

diphtheria—A serious bacterial infection usually affecting the mucous membranes of your nose and throat.

exhume—To dig out something buried, especially a corpse from the ground.

Lucha Libre—A type of professional wrestling originating in Mexico.

masochism—The tendency to derive pleasure, especially sexual gratification, from one's own pain or humiliation.

obsessive compulsive disorder (OCD)— An anxiety disorder that is characterized by recurrent, unwanted thoughts—obsessions—and repetitive behaviors.

pedophile—A person who is sexually attracted to children.

perversion—A sexual behavior or desire that is considered abnormal or unacceptable.

psychiatry—The study and treatment of mental illness, emotional disturbance, and abnormal behavior.

psychology—The scientific study of the human mind and its functions, especially those affecting behavior in a given context.

sadism—The tendency to derive pleasure, especially sexual gratification, from inflicting pain, suffering, or humiliation on others.

sadomasochism—A psychological tendency or sexual practice characterized by both sadism and masochism.

strychnine—A highly toxic, colorless, odorless, bitter crystalline powder used as a pesticide.

toxicology—The branch of science concerned with the nature, effects, and detection of poisons.

tuberculosis—A potentially fatal contagious disease that can affect almost any part of the body but is mainly an infection of the lungs. It is caused by a bacterial microorganism, *tubercle bacillus* or *Mycobacterium tuberculosis*.

Further Reading

Books

Houck, Max M., and Jay A. Siegel. *Fundamentals of Forensic Science*. San Diego, CA.: Academic Press/Elsevier, 2015.

Lightning Guides Editors. *Serial Killers: Jack the Ripper to The Zodiac Killer*. Berkeley, CA.: Lightning Guides/Callisto Media, 2015.

Parker, R.J. *The Serial Killer Compendium*. Seattle, Wash.: CreateSpace Independent Publishing, 2012.

Raine, Adrian. *The Anatomy of Violence: The Psychological Roots of Crime*. New York: Vintage, 2014.

Ronson, Jan. *The Psychopath Test: A Journey Through the Madness Industry*. New York: Penguin Publishing, 2012.

Slate, J.J. *Serial Killers* (Encyclopedia of 100 Serial Killers). Toronto, Ontario, Canada: R.J. Parker Publishing, 2014.

Websites

Murderpedia
murderpedia.org
Murderpedia is the world's largest database of serial killers.

The Serial Killer Database Research Project
skdb.fgcu.edu/info.asp
The Serial Killer Database Research Project collects data on serial killers and presents public statistics.

Videos

Aileen Wuornos: The Selling of a Serial Killer.
Directed by Nick Broomfield. 1993.
Appropriate Adult. (TV miniseries)
Directed by Julian Jarrold. 2011.

Index